T0082429

In Frederic Hunter's novel *The Congo Prophet*, we are in the Belgian Congo in 1921. Maurice Count Lippens, the newly appointed governor-general, has been sent to establish a new, civilized regime—just 13 years after the end of the Congo Free State where King Leopold II exploited and terrorized the people. Lippens has good intentions, yet reforming an administration previously used to oppress Africans is much more difficult than it sounds. Belgium rules millions of Congolese with only a few thousand administrators, plus the Force Publique, the Army that provides policing to the colony. The key stakeholders are the Roman Catholic church, Protestant missionaries, Belgian settlers, and the administration.

Confronted with a Congolese healer who has inspired thousands to leave their homes, the stakeholders all want the healer killed, so that the situation can go back to normal. However, the healer has broken no laws.

This is the dilemma that faces Count Lippens. How can he be expected to bring the rule of law to a broken country?

The Congo Prophet brilliantly portrays the dilemmas of colonial administration, the rule of law, and the meaning of justice.

—Ted Anagnoson, Professor Emeritus, Political Science,
Cal State Los Angeles.

I would like to thank my wife Donanne, my son Paul, and the crew at Cune Press for their help in bringing this book into being.
—Frederic Hunter

CONGO PROPHET

A NOVEL

Frederic Hunter

Cune

Congo Prophet: A Novel
by Fredric Hunter
© 2022 Frederic Hunter
Cune Press, Seattle 2022

Hardback	ISBN 9781951082727
Paperback	ISBN 9781951082222
EPUB	ISBN 9781614574286
Kindle	ISBN 9781614572602

Library of Congress Cataloging-in-Publication Data

Names: Hunter, Frederic, author.
Title: Congo prophet : the arrest of Simon Kimbangu / a novel by Frederic Hunter.
Other titles: Bridge between the cultures series.
Description: Seattle : Cune Press, 2022. | Series: Bridge between the cultures
Identifiers: LCCN 2022014142 (print) | LCCN 2022014143 (ebook) | ISBN
    9781951082222 (trade paperback) | ISBN 9781614574286 (epub)
Subjects: LCSH: Kimbangu, Simon, 1887-1951--Fiction. | Congo (Democratic Republic)--Fiction.
Classification: LCC PS3558.U477 C66 2022 (print) | LCC PS3558.U477
    (ebook) | DDC 813.54--dc23/eng/20220323
LC record available at https://lccn.loc.gov/2022014142
LC ebook record available at https://lccn.loc.gov/2022014143
CP 09012022.

Note on Naming: This book concerns the Democratic Republic of the Congo, sometimes referred to as Congo-Kinshasa, DR Congo, the DRC, the DROC or the Congo (before 1997 called "Zaire").

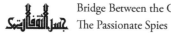

Bridge Between the Cultures (a series from Cune Press)

The Passionate Spies	John Harte
Music Has No Boundaries	Rafiq Gangat
Arab Boy Delivered	Paul Aziz Zarou
Kivu	Frederic Hunter
Empower a Refugee	Patricia Martin Holt
Afghanistan and Beyond	Linda Sartor
The Greatest Spy	John Harte
Stories My Father Told Me	Helen Zughaib, Elia Zughaib
Apartheid Is a Crime	Mats Svensson
Definitely Maybe Not	Stephen Fife
Girl Fighters	Carolyn Han
White Carnations	Musa Rahum Abbas

 Cune Press: www.cunepress.com | www.cunepress.net

The African Continent

Lower Congo

Leopoldville
(Kinshasa)

Boma

Thysville
(Mbanza-Ngungu)

Bakongo
People Area

The colonial administration when Count Lippens arrived in the Congo in 1921 was still based in Boma in the Congo delta (later moved upriver to Leopoldville / Kinshasha).

Simon was born at Nhamba near Thysville (Mbanza-Ngungu) in 1887 and lived among the Bakongo people. Later, he was incarcerated by the Belgians and moved in shackles to the far eastern part of Congo where he was imprisoned for life in Elisabethville (Lumbashi).

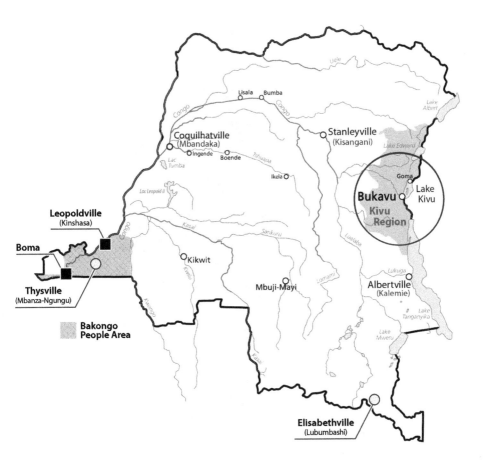

Note that Frederic Hunter's recent memoir *Kivu* is set in the shaded area near Bukavu as shown to the north and east of the area where Simon lived and was imprisoned.

Hunter's forthcoming memoir *Equateur: A Year at the Edge of the Jungle* is set in Coquilhatville, roughly halfway between the delta country where Simon was born and the eastern region of Kivu.

Count Maurice Lippens was born into a progressive Belgian family in 1875 and installed as Governor-General of the Belgian Congo in 1921. Lippens was quick to launch major administrative reforms. However, he met resistance from the Belgian colonial administration and quit his post in 1923.

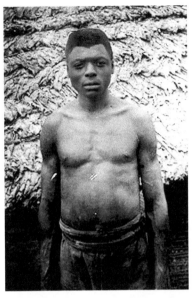

Simon Kimbangu was born into a traditional religious family in 1887, became a Baptist in 1915, and began his own religious practice in 1921. According to his followers, Simon raised the dead, healed the sick, foretold the future, and saw a time when black Congolese would rule themselves.

Simon was captured by the Belgian authorities in the Congo in 1921 and died in captivity in 1951.

ONE

BEFORE THE APPOINTMENT WAS ANNOUNCED to the public, Maurice Count Lippens and his wife Joanna invited members of the family to a soirée at their home. After enjoying wine and a five-course candle-lit dinner, family members learned the good news. Shouting approval, they toasted the couple and basked in the sense that positive developments lay ahead both for the Count and for that exotic and resource-rich stretch of green wilderness where he would hold sway. It lay a little less far away than the moon. Count Lippens had just been named Governor-General of the Belgian Congo.

The family dining room rang with congratulations. But there was also a challenge. Toward the end of the dinner Countess Joanna's brother Hugo shouted, "Why Africa? I thought you were doing well as governor of East Flanders."

"He is," replied Countess Joanna, an edge in her voice. It was often necessary to let an edge creep into one's voice when dealing with Hugo.

"Then why let them rusticate you to nowhere?" Hugo demanded.

"It's not rustication," answered the Count mildly. "It's a promotion."

"East Flanders is a mere province," explained the Countess rather testily. "The Congo is a vast stretch—"

"Of nowhere!" replied her brother.

"It's the Belgian bureaucracy's highest position," said the Countess.

"Impossible!" insisted the contrarian brother. "A bureaucrat wants to stay close to the center of power. That's the palace in Brussels. It's not a grass hut in the Congo!"

Family members felt embarrassed by this challenge.

"The Congo is a terrible place," argued Hugo. "We send young men out there who risk dying to become rich. The lucky ones don't die. They go insane with loneliness, take black companions and breed picannins. The unlucky ones die anyway, sometimes felled by dread diseases, sometimes by their own hands."

"I don't expect to do either," observed the Count.

"In addition, Maurice," charged Hugo, "you'll become a murderer."

The Count smiled tolerantly. "I hardly think so," he said.

"Murder is the colonial policy," insisted his brother-in-law. "You'll--"

"Hugo, my dear," the Count's mother interrupted, "please don't ruin this lovely dinner. I'm sure you were brought up knowing that a guest does not argue with his host."

Hugo bowed his head deferentially to his brother-in-law's mother and held his peace.

Held it at least until the party broke up and most of the guests had departed. As Hugo was saying goodnight, his sister implored, "Please, brother. Bid us success in the Congo."

"Of course," he said. "May you turn it into a model colony." He kissed her cheek. But before actually leaving, he could not stop himself from giving vent to what he actually thought. "I'm sorry," he excused himself, "but I must say this. Maurice, why are you associating yourself with that pestiferous place? King Leopold was an infamous scoundrel, a murderer. His freebooters were second-raters out for plunder. They killed hundreds of thousands of poor Africans to pay for the colony and make Leopold rich. Really! Stay away from that place!"

"I agree with you about Leopold," the Count acknowledged. "But someone needs to set the colony straight and repair our international reputation."

"Don't you see?" demanded the Countess. "It's an extraordinary opportunity. Beside it, East Flanders is nothing."

"But how an opportunity?" demanded her brother. "Do you realize there's hardly a Governor-General known to history. Only one: Pontius Pilate!"

The Count and his wife burst out laughing. Hugo was laughing, too. Still, he cried, "I'm serious! Pilate allowed bureaucracy to make him a murderer. And how does history remember him?" asked Hugo. "As even worse than Leopold."

By now they were all laughing.

The Countess noted, "Maurice does not intend to execute anyone. So there!" She pushed her brother out the door.

This soiree occurred in late 1920. King Leopold II's rule in the Congo Free State had ended. Still, the scandal it provoked remained fresh in people's minds. The king had first held the territory as his personal fief. Instead of pouring enlightenment and investment money into the colony, as he had promised, he and the men he sent to administer it sought to wring riches from it. Instead of ridding the territory of the slave trade – he had promised that, too – Leopold allowed his freebooters to act as slavers themselves. They exploited native labor with such cruelty that they claimed the lives of millions of Congolese. They set quotas of wild rubber that village men would gather. They held hostage the women and children of those villages. Starvation resulted. The African population plummeted.

The freebooters also slaughtered thousands of elephants for their ivory.

Belgium became a pariah in the world. In 1908 the king's infamy caused the Belgian people to wrest control of the Congo Free State from him.

Setting the colony on a new course and, as a result, helping to restore Belgium's standing in the world would not be easily done. Count Lippens often wondered privately to himself – he did not share these musings - if he was truly the right man for the job. After all, Leopold was still revered by many with influence at the palace. The new appointment, however, deeply pleased the Lippens family. Its members prided themselves in the family's reputation for service to the country. And now the Count had ascended to its highest post.

The Count was tall and fair with patrician good looks. In a full dress uniform with studded epaulets and medals hanging from his broad chest, a wide ribbon stretching across it from his shoulder to his waist, he appeared to merit the trust of those he governed.

Born in Ghent, he grew up speaking both Flemish and French. He spent three years of the Great War in a German prison camp. After the war he served his country as Governor of East Flanders. He was now forty-five.

His wife Joanna was a beauty. Almost a decade younger, she possessed curiosity, an irreverent sense of humor, and a readiness for adventure that would serve her well in a country so strange to them. These traits boded well for them in their new home.

Count Maurice had never taken lightly the good fortune of being born a Lippens. He had modeled himself after his father Hippolyte, who, for a dozen years, had been mayor of Ghent. Hippolyte Lippens long felt that the nobility had an obligation to support the king, even if at the beginning of the twentieth century kingship seemed out-of-date. He admired King Leopold II as a Man of Big Ideas, a monarch intent on carving out a place in the world for tiny Belgium despite a lack of financial resources, despite a population indifferent to Big Ideas.

Since in the late nineteenth century Leopold was highly respected throughout Europe as a philanthropic monarch. So it was not difficult for Hippolyte to support the king. Leopold seemed intent on spending much of his personal fortune to send troops to rid the Congo Free State of slave-traders. He also encouraged Christian missionaries to civilize the populations of the Dark Continent.

When Hippolyte Lippens was offered a position on the administrative board of the *Comité du Congo pour le Commerce et l'Industrie*, he accepted it as a way of showing solidarity with Leopold's philanthropic efforts.

In far-away Europe it had been difficult for Hippolyte Lippens actually to conceive of the Congo Free State's African populations. They were black as night. While they could fight fiercely, they could neither read nor write. Some went about literally naked. Primitive, uncivilized, they seemed sub-human, not like brother men. It was easiest to regard them as savages, almost as beasts.

There were whispers that the men who tried to civilize these populations treated them roughly. Hippolyte shrugged off such rumors. Leopold's good works could not succeed if done with kid gloves. One must break a few eggs to make an omelette.

At Hippolyte's death, Maurice Lippens became count. He also inherited both his father's place on CCCI's administrative board and his unchallenged attitudes about the Free State populations. Soon, however, he heard rumblings about the way the savage populations were worked, forced to gather wild rubber. If the quotas were not filled, punishments were inflicted. Villagers were killed.

Count Maurice read a report about an area where wild rubber vines were picked clean. Desperate workers rebelled against the freebooters' punishments. They killed thirty soldiers. Other soldiers mounted a punitive expedition against them. More villagers were killed, their families left to suffer. The Count wondered about such reports. But being both young and the new man on the CCCI board, he did not feel himself in a position to investigate such reports.

Then the friend who tutored him in English gave him a short novel to read: Joseph Conrad's *Heart of Darkness*. The Count did not read it to its end. Compelling, yes, but full of exaggerations. How could it be true? That Kurtz, the chief of the Inner Station, surrounded his house with posts on which he fixed the heads of slain Africans? Surely that was far-fetched. Kurtz's exotic African woman made the tale intriguing. The Count had heard of her. She gave the story erotic sizzle. But obviously Conrad had imagined her. Surely such women did not roam the Free State bush.

The Count heard rumors of atrocity reports sent to the British Foreign Office by their consul in the Congo, the Irishman Roger Casement. He learned of accusations made by the Brit J. D. Morel and his Congo Reform Association. The charges seemed hysterical.

Since the British wanted to extend their holdings in Africa, their reports of atrocities were suspect. Casement and Morel might well be unreliable. It was not surprising that the ruling elites of competing colonial powers should attempt to besmirch Leopold's Free State achievements and connive to pick off parts of its territory.

Then the Count saw photographs taken in Leopold's Free State: children without hands. Taskmasters had chopped them off. Black boys of seven or eight stared out of the photographs. The Count found the images deeply disturbing. He had children only a little bit older. He could not look at the photographs. Yet at the same time he could hardly lift his eyes from them. The black boys spoke to him from them; they asked him to recognize their humanity.

A realization struck the Count. The Congo's dark populations were not sub-human. They were not mere beasts. These boys without hands... How did they feed themselves? How did they urinate? How did they wipe themselves clean after defecating? How did they accomplish tasks?

These boys were not savages. They belonged not to the Free State, but to their parents, men and women like the Count and his wife. These black people lived in families. The parents treasured their children and wanted them to prosper, not to be maimed by sadists.

The photographs rendered atrocities in the Congo undeniable. Now it was impossible for Maurice Count Lippens to admire King Leopold II as his father had done. Now he realized the truth of the rumors he had heard. Instead of pouring investment money into the colony as he had promised, the king and the men he sent to administer it exploited native labor with undeniable cruelty.

The Count was grateful when Belgians throughout the country became so embarrassed by their king that they forced Leopold to cede the Free State to Belgium.

Shortly thereafter the Great War occurred. During the German occupation of Belgium Count Lippens joined the resistance and was caught. Germans imprisoned him from 1915 to 1918. In 1919 he was appointed Governor of the Belgian Province of East Flanders. With a flair for organization, he undertook improvements to provincial education and health care.

Less than two years later the Minister of Colonies asked to meet with the Count. Whatever in the world for, wondered the Count. At their meeting they talked about Africa, the Belgian Congo. Did it interest him? Had he ever thought of going there? Would he perhaps be interested in becoming the colony's Governor-General?

The Count swore almost inaudibly under his breath. "Governor-General of the Belgian Congo?" He stared with disbelief at the Minister of Colonies.

"How could I possibly consider that?" he asked. "I've had no experience of Africa. In any case I haven't been in East Flanders long enough to finish the work I need to do there."

The Minister shrugged. He did not need to explain that the Governor-Generalship was immeasurably more important than a stretch of Flanders.

"Anyway," said the Count, "isn't that position generally filled by men who've served out there?"

"The palace thinks new approaches ought to be tried," said the Minister. "The structure of the administration needs reformation. They think you're the man to do it."

The Count stared across the room, not looking at his companion.

"Nothing is more important than our work in the Congo," noted the Minister. "The taint of the Free State still has to be removed."

The Count asked for several days to consider the matter.

Setting the colony on a new course would not be easy. Its territory was forty times, no, sixty times larger than-- Who really knew how much larger, how much more populous it was than Belgium? It was almost larger than Europe. It had rain forests in the north, savannas in the south, glacier-clad peaks in the northeast. A huge river, larger and flowing faster than any in Europe, surged through it. A range of treacherous mountains in the southwest thwarted, but did not stop, the river's quest to reach the sea. The Count knew that many men had died building a railroad across those mountains from the Atlantic Ocean.

After doing some investigation he discovered that the people of the colony numbered in the millions. There were large tribal groups living, highly organized, in savanna urban collectivities. There were also pygmies living in isolated forest villages without any tribal organization at all. Where there were tribes - perhaps two hundred of them - there were tribal rivalries. Where there were different languages – at least as many as the different tribes – there were misunderstandings.

Misunderstandings, even violence, had forged the colony. Famed explorer Henry Morton Stanley had sailed down the Congo River at Leopold's behest, shooting at any Africans who scowled at him, stopping to make treaties with those who didn't scowl.

To Africans who had never seen either paper or writing, he presented contracts that ceded their lands to the king. He explained the stipulations they were accepting in a language the Africans did not understand. Greedy colonizing nations honored such treaties as if they represented genuine contracts with the riverside chieftains whom Stanley assisted in making their marks.

It was no surprise that reforms needed to be made. But did Count Lippens want to undertake the challenge? When he conferred with his wife, she did not say, "Horrors! I wouldn't think of it." She congratulated him on what would be a significant promotion and observed that if he declined the post, such an opportunity might never be offered again.

As she considered the new assignment, the Countess developed a little narrative about what would happen to the couple if they went to Africa. They were good people. They had solid Belgian values and the best of intentions. They had discretion. They would work hard. They would identify and cultivate influential individuals and bring progress. When she thought of these individuals, they were always whites, settlers. When she saw photographs of Africans, it did not occur to her that black people could be cultivated. How could that possibly happen?

They would leave their children – three of them – in Belgium under the care of the count's mother. That would be hard, but at the end of two years, maybe five, according to her narrative, the Lippenses would have served Belgium nobly. They would have set the colony on a new course. They would have begun restoring the administration's reputation.

The Count was interested in decentralizing power from the capital at Boma to the provinces. He would institute budgetary and educational reforms. When the couple returned to Belgium, rewards would await them. The Countess did not know what rewards they would actually be; time would reveal them.

The Count doubted that things would unfold quite the way his wife envisioned them. After all, they had no idea what awaited them in Africa. But he was by nature optimistic. So the notion that her narrative should come to pass seemed at least within the realm of possibility.

However he warned her, "It could be very primitive out there."

"What do you think?" she asked. "We want to think of your advancement, don't we?" When the Count did not immediately reply, she added, "Your family has always served the country."

At that moment in his mind's eye the Count saw the two Congolese boys staring at him out of the photograph, showing the stumps of their arms without hands. Were they asking him to help them?

"It's a significant advance over East Flanders," said the Countess. "The palace has its eye on you."

"I do not think a rational man would take this job," observed the Count.

"But you know how profoundly I was affected by the photo—"

"Of the two boys," said the Countess . "Yes, I know."

"It made me a different person somehow."

"You cannot give them back their hands, you know."

"But there are things we could do. Improvements we could make."

For Belgium they agreed to give Africa a try.

TWO

COUNT AND COUNTESS LIPPENS SAILED FROM Antwerp in February, 1921. They left behind wintry Belgium with its wan light, its overcast, the occasional snow flurries and what its own citizens acknowledged was a mercantile mentality. They voyaged down the Channel, past Britain and La Belle France and out into the Atlantic. They passed Spain, the Pillars of Hercules, and headed for the Canary Islands.

The voyage was long. The Count occupied himself reading briefing materials about the colony, about the thirty-five hundred Belgian settlers who looked to the colonial administration for protection and the betterment of their lives, about the uncounted millions of Africans, black people so different from anyone he had ever known. He read statements of Belgian colonial ideology; they boiled down to: "Rule to serve." That sounded high-minded, but, thought the Count, rather too much like the promises Leopold made, on which he never delivered.

Ruling to serve was to be achieved on the three legs of a stool: technical progress, the introduction of Christianity, and projects for the betterment of native welfare. To achieve this last he was charged with reforming the *chefferie* system under which they lived.

He could not study without a break, especially when ideology inflamed his skepticism. At the insistence of the Countess, he socialized with passengers. He played cards and quoits. He circumnavigated the deck. He stared at the open sea. One day he saw flying fish. The next it was a school of dolphins. They jumped through the waves with such beauty that he rushed to the railing to watch them. He hoped to see a whale, but none appeared during the voyage.

One evening after dinner he found himself in the ship's small library. He did not want to read the romances or mysteries with which his wife was passing her time. The more serious fare was outdated. In a library where virtually everything was in French he came upon a thin volume undoubtedly left behind by an English-speaking passenger: *Heart of Darkness* by Joseph Conrad. It was the story he had declined to finish a year or two earlier when his English tutor presented it to him. Hmm, thought the Count. The tutor had suggested that it would challenge his English vocabulary and might offend his Belgian identity. He passed on finishing it at the time. He never expected to become involved in the Congo.

Now things were different. He had time to spend with a book that would test his English. More importantly he was interested in Conrad's impressions of Leopold's Free State thirty years earlier. He recalled that Conrad had experienced a very rough passage in the Free State, that he described it as a place of darkness, corruption, and venality. His time there had badly damaged his health.

Forewarned, the Count opened the book and started to read.

It was hard going. The sentences struck him as long and convoluted. They seemed as thick with big words as the Congo jungle was reported to be thick with undergrowth. It seemed to take Conrad forever to introduce the reader to Marlow, his alter ego, and start the tale of his journey. Initially it took him to what was obviously Brussels, described by Marlow as a city of "whited sepulchers." The Count wondered exactly what that meant, a place of hypocrisy apparently.

He read for more than an hour. Marlow/Conrad arrived in the Free State of 1889. The landscape struck him as suggesting the beginnings of time. Then the Count came upon a paragraph that made him laugh. He thought he must share the joke with the Countess and went out onto the deck where she was sitting in a deckchair watching the ocean.

The Count could not at first locate his wife because where she had been sitting solitary, there were now two chairs together drawn up before the railing, a couple occupying them, the man holding a cigarillo in his left hand, away from his companion. The Count halted for a moment in confusion. He heard the man's spirited laughter, that of a young man apparently engaged in charming his companion.

Suddenly the Count realized that the man's companion was his wife. The Count smiled to himself, realizing that his wife might be enjoying the young man's attention. It appeared to be a kind of flirtation. He observed the couple for several moments, wondering if he should return to the library and not interrupt the proceedings. Then the young man hurled his cigarillo overboard and turned on the chair, perching on its edge facing the Countess. Time to intrude, judged the Count. He moved toward the couple, exclaiming, "Ah, my dear, I have found something to read, and I see you've found a fellow passenger."

The young man stood and introduced himself as Antoine Sambry. "My friends call me Tony," he said, "and I hope you will."

"Are you bound for the Congo?" asked the Count.

"Indeed, I am," said Sambry. "I'm seeking my fortune among the blacks.

I've joined the colonial service for three years. Time enough to investigate Africa's possibilities, maybe discover a gold mine, collect some ivory, or establish a plantation."

"Why not all three?" suggested the Count.

"Good idea!" replied Sambry. "After a decade. I'll return to Europe dripping riches and marry a regal virgin who will recognize an adventurer and fall in love with me at first sight." He laughed, pleased with himself.

The Count judged that his mustaches and goatee were newly grown and that he was probably not older than twenty-five. "That's quite a plan," commented the Count.

"To attack the jungle one needs a plan," noted the young man.

The Count suspected that their new friend Tony had probably not attacked the delectable older woman without a plan.

"The newly appointed Governor-General is on board," commented the young man. "I think I've seen him: a pompous-looking graybeard pacing the decks. I'm sure that's him. Perhaps I should introduce myself. Can't do any harm to know the Gov-Gen."

"Do that!" urged the Countess. "Nice to have met you."

"Offer him one of your cigars," suggested the Count. He and young Sambry shook hands and the young man went off to find the pompous old deck-walker.

The Count settled himself in the deck chair that Sambry had warmed for him. "Nice to have you meeting new people," he told his wife. "You didn't tell him who you were?"

"Too busy talking about himself. Do you think he'll make a successful territorial administrator?"

"Perhaps he'll find that gold mine. There are plenty of unexplored minerals in the Congo." The Count looked at the ocean. Then he added, "Or perhaps he'll disappear into the vastness of Africa and will never be heard from again."

"I suspect he's not the type one doesn't hear about."

After a moment the Count remarked, "You know, he was angling to take you to bed."

The Countess tossed her husband a look. "An old lady like me?"

"Who better for a shipboard romance? 'Old ladies' know the tricks."

"This old lady knows only those you taught me." She added, "The question is: Who taught you?"

They laughed together. "Time to change the subject," said the Count. "I found something to read in the library." He told his wife about his discovery.

"It won't keep you awake at night, will it?"

"We are lucky to be going out there thirty years after Conrad visited the place. He wasn't fond of it." The Count stared at the ocean and slapped the small volume against his hand. "A lot of men died out there in his day. Fellows like your friend who went to seek their fortune."

While the Countess watched the ocean, the Count read her the passage from *Heart of Darkness* that amused him. Marlow/Conrad was relating the vicissitudes of venturing up the Congo River. "I managed not to sink that steamboat on my first trip." He read. "It's a wonder to me yet. Imagine a blindfolded man set to drive a van over a bad road."

"That made you laugh?" asked the Countess.

"Don't you see? I'm the blindfolded man, trying not to sink the ship."

"You will do fine, my dear. Even if you do mix your metaphors." She reached over to take his hand and winked at him. "You know all the tricks."

After a landfall in the Canaries, the skies cleared. The sun beat down. The reserve of Europe, of winter, gave way to the music and laughter of sunshine. The Count studied official reports and dipped into Conrad in a deck chair.

The ship's passengers were not so numerous that he could not observe those who voyaged with him and the Countess. He easily identified the "pompous graybeard" that Sambry had assumed was the Governor-General; he made his acquaintance. His wife befriended a young woman, rather plain, traveling alone. When the Countess presented her, the Count discovered that she was en route to the Congo to marry an officer in the colonial service.

Several young men were traveling to the Congo to take up posts as colonial officers. Feeling a fatherly interest in these young men, the Count observed them, understanding that they would represent the colony in what might be remote, even solitary, posts. He wondered how well they would perform, understanding that their performance could lead to successes that would make his job easier or to problems that might lead to trouble.

One forenoon as the Count and his wife relaxed in their deck chairs Sambry bounded up to them, laughing. "My regrets, Excellency," he enthused. "I apologize for treating you so casually when we met. I've discovered who you are."

"Won't you join us?" suggested the Count. "Tell us what else you've learned on the voyage."

The young man pulled a deck chair up beside the couple and settled into it. The Count asked him what had attracted him to the colonial service. "The opportunities!" he exclaimed. "They're so great. The kind of life that was my destiny had I stayed in Belgium was very clear to me. I would marry a tedious woman I had known since I was five. The career I would have was already marked out. So boring it made me shudder. I ran away to Paris for a while. But I couldn't afford that place. Knew I must leave Europe."

The Count asked if the other young passengers bound for the colonial service felt the same way. Sambry assured him that they all had had similar experiences.

"I have been reading a story about the Free State," said the Count, "by a man who went out there thirty years ago. He did not like it at all. In fact, he lost his health there. Do you and your friends know the dangers that may be ahead of you?"

Sambry laughed. "Bring on the dangers!" he exclaimed. "Our lives in Belgium were so safe!"

The Count laughed with him. He had been feeling some responsibility about protecting the newcomers to his colonial service and realized that he need not worry about that. He asked Sambry to introduce him to his friends and the Count soon made their acquaintance. Sambry appeared to be the most venturesome of the bunch, as if 'dangers' were his destiny.

The Count observed Sambry and his pals, trying to assess their qualities. His wife kept an eye on the young woman going to the Congo to marry an officer serving there.

On the deck one afternoon, the Count noticed Sambry and this young woman in deckchairs studying the ocean together. Sambry was bantering with her in much the same way the Count had seen him bantering with his wife. The woman obviously enjoyed his attention. On another occasion he saw them circumnavigating the deck together. Walking behind them, he watched Sambry pull her off the deck into a hallway of staterooms. Hmm, he thought. A shipboard romance? Perhaps, perhaps not. On a long voyage, shouldn't young people find friends?

The Count and his wife crossed the Equator. They tolerated, even enjoyed, the antics of the sailors initiating passengers into the southern hemisphere. These antics broke the tedium of the trip. The Count had begun to spend a great deal of time, pacing about the decks. He was impatient for the trip to end, ready to begin his job.

Late one evening after prowling the decks, he sat alone in a corner of the saloon, reading papers picked up in Dakar, wanting to be alone. His wife felt ill and retired. Sambry and another young man bound for the Congo were drinking together across the room, so close to being drunk that they were unaware of the Count. They laughed together, occasionally bursting into song and conversing loud enough for the Count to overhear.

"The blacks are so ugly," complained Sambry's companion. That made the Count prick up his ears. "Have you seen photographs? Savages! Bones in their noses. Scars on their faces. Disfigure their ear lobes, their mouths. Can you imagine romancing a dusky maiden?"

"With no trouble at all," chuckled Sambry. He burst into song, laughed heartily, and vowed, "Now and then I expect to come upon one I could fancy."

"I'm not counting on it."

"You not an explorer, eh?" questioned Sambry. He lowered his voice. But the Count still followed what was said. "I don't know about you, but I'm used to getting it at least once a week."

The companion chuckled and said, "Good luck on that."

"Free most of the time," boasted Sambry. "But I'm not above paying. Don't expect to get along without it."

"I'm thinking my hand will be busy." His companion giggled. "In fact, it already has been."

"I keep wondering," confessed Sambry. "If you sleep with a savage, does the black rub off?" The companion snickered. "Do you rise up, your body blackened? Does your wick come out black?"

The companion tittered. "Mine may go black if I pound it too often."

"Mine," Sambry speculated, "may go black from overuse." The companion shook his head and slapped his knee. "That would be inconvenient to explain to nubile virgins when I get home."

"I'll check on you in six months."

"Mine may be tattooed by then." The two men bent over to suppress their giggles. The Count smiled to himself behind his newspaper.

As the ship moved south, the Count studied clouds far out across the ocean. Sometimes the sky was overcast and the gray days depressing. Sometimes rain fell on and on in great sheets. Imprisoned in his stateroom, the Count studied reports. He finished Conrad's *Heart of Darkness*, met Mr. Kurtz, attended his death, and confronted his last words, "The horror, the horror!" He wondered what that was all about. The venality of the Free State? The corruption of the enterprise? Kurtz's guilt at the slaughter of elephants? Or the hypocrisy of the lies he had allowed to shape his destiny?

Having finished the story, the Count walked about the deck in blazing sunlight. He hoped he himself would not want to cry those words at the end of his stint in the Congo. Occasionally he wondered what had possessed him to agree to become the colony's Governor-General. Vanity? He did not think so. He was not vain. Ambition? No. Ambition would have advised him to stay close to the palace in Brussels. A sense of purpose? Probably. Although he did not finish the work he set for himself in East Flanders, he thought he could do a good work for his country in the Belgian Congo despite having no experience of colonies or of Africa.

He took a deck chair and wondered about that purpose. What exactly was it? He did not think of himself as a creature of Belgian colonialism, that compromised system, although he had become one. Nor did he think of himself as a colonial bureaucrat, although he had also become one of those. His purpose had been merely to be a good Belgian, a lawyer, a businessman, an able governor, rendering a service to his country.

The Count knew that, given unlucky circumstances, a foreign administrator was certain to face pressures from contending interest groups. He himself would do his best to manage pressure in an enlightened way. Might there be accusations brought against agents like Kurtz? Or colonial officers like Sambry, however they turned out? How would he handle them? Would he be able to read the nuances of such situations, situations he might not fully understand? Congolese were certain to produce unexpected problems. He could not imagine what they might be. What then?

He wondered: Would he be strong enough to withstand extreme pressures marshaled against him? From settlers? From the Catholic Church which would expect special treatment? From Protestant missionaries who would demand a measure of fairness? From the black masses of Congolese who would expect better treatment than they had received in the Free State era? In his deck chair the Count stared at the ocean and hoped that he would not face too much that was tricky.

He did not minimize how frightened he might be in the face of rebellion, standing against thousands of blacks, shouting, and holding spears, their drums beating savage rhythms, their magic arrayed against him, and all the while settlers demanding military action against them.

The Countess came and took the deckchair beside him. "I've ordered us tea," she said.

"Good. I'd like some tea."

"You thinking lofty thoughts?"

"Just watching clouds."

The Countess studied his face. She reached out and took his hand. "My dear," she said, "I can see that it's more than clouds. Something's bothering you."

"You have known me too long."

"Tell me about it."

The refreshments arrived. The Countess poured tea for both of them, set cake beside each cup and handed a plate to her husband. He drank and watched the ocean. Finally he said, "I've been wondering why I took this job that has thrust us into something we know too little about, that has caused us to leave our children in my mother's care."

The Countess laughed. "We may all love each other more for the separation. Maybe they can join us for school holidays."

They drank tea and observed the ocean. The Countess refilled their cups and offered her husband more cake.

The Count said, "I wonder if I can really start to change the mentality of the whites we'll encounter. There was so much death in the Free State era. Reading that fool story reminded me of that."

They drank tea for a time without speaking. Finally the Count remarked, "I'm quite intent on making the administration more effective, more humane. It cries out for that after the excesses of the Free State. I'm happy to encourage the Katanga mines to produce more ore to make Belgians rich so long as they improve their workers' conditions. And to do what I can to encourage completion of the Matadi-Kinshasa Railway."

He continued, "I'm aware that some of our companies – the wild rubber people and the palm nut gatherers – probably overwork their laborers in conditions that speed their deaths. Those conditions must be improved."

"You've been worried about that?"

The Count shrugged. "When will this voyage end?" He drank his tea and looked out at the endless ocean.

THREE

ONE MORNING, NEARING THEIR DESTINATION, the Count observed a current of muddy water flowing in the dark sea. "That's the Congo River," said the vessel's captain. "It's been carrying silt all the way from the center of Africa. Now it's muscling its way into the ocean, saying, 'Here I come! Make way for me!'" The Count wondered if that was how things were done in Africa: muscling one's way. That was certainly how Henry Morton Stanley had done things.

As the ship drew closer to land, the Count saw that the silt's color grew ever darker. What at his first notice had seemed only a flow became a surge, an indomitable, unstoppable onrush. Watching it push quieter waters out of its way, the Count received his first impression of the power he would encounter in Africa. And the size of things. What power! What size! In Europe he had never known a river of such width and thrust. Moreover, the sun seemed twice as large as any sun he had ever seen in Flanders. It hung twice as close to the earth.

The Count and his Countess made their way up the estuary of the great river to Boma, the capital of the Belgian Congo. En route there Lippens received other impressions: the strength of the sun, its brilliance, its glare, its relentlessness beating down. And the power of green, the multiplicity of greenish hues surrounding them, soothing them, a power of reassurance after the hustle and traffic of the cities of the North.

There were also sense impressions that almost overwhelmed them: the warmth and humidity of the air, the verdant lushness of the vegetation, the chirruping of crickets and a constant croaking of frogs, the taste and profusion of fruits they had always regarded as exotic: bananas, mangoes, pineapples, papayas. There was the smell of burning vegetation carried by breezes from nearby villages where black people went about virtually unclothed and cooked over open fires. That nakedness! Nearly naked people, black as night, living in villages of huts made of grass. The sight of those villages perplexed, but also rather charmed, the couple.

When their ship docked at Boma, a salute by cannon fire from the fort welcomed the new arrivals. So did drumming by a group of natives. A greeting committee of colonial officials waited on the dock. In white uniforms and pith helmets, they seemed almost to shine. The Governor-General's aide, an

27

"old hand" in the colony although only in his mid-thirties, stepped forward to take charge of arrangements. He was Willem Van Belle, like the Count of Flemish background, but with ten years experience in the colony.

Boma made the Lippenses aware that they had arrived in a different world, in Africa, in the Congo. The town, quite rustic it seemed to them, lay on ground that stretched between docks on the mighty river and the uprise of land behind it. On this ground colonials had built the warehouses of trading companies, a Force Publique fort, a hospital for Europeans, a post office, a hotel with dining room, bar, and other amenities for the variety of beings, mostly men, who passed through. There was also a church, called "the cathedral" since Boma was the capital of the colony.

The newcomers boarded a trolley that moved them through a banana plantation and lifted them out of the town up to a plateau where Van Belle pointed out government offices and the houses of the officials who worked in them. "It's cooler up here," he noted.

"Yes," said the Countess with a grateful smile.

Van Belle led them to a Victorian mansion – cupola, covered porches, French windows, exterior staircases – the residence of the Governor-General. Force Publique sentries stood guard before it. The Count would never think of it as the "palace," although some of the colonials did.

As they approached it, the couple exchanged a glance. Raising an eyebrow to her husband, the Countess gestured that the mansion, however grand it was for Boma, represented a comedown from their home in Ghent They climbed the steep steps to the entrance. They halted on the balcony to survey the river, the town, and jungle below, then made their way into their new home. Van Belle introduced Count and Countess Lippens to their servants and made sure the luggage arrived.

The rooms were large. Overstuffed, Belgian-style furniture of local manufacture crowded the parlor. Rotating fans hung from high ceilings. The official dining room seemed to stretch forever. Its walls displayed paintings of Belgium probably executed by homesick settlers. The Countess wondered what kind of dinner parties she would be expected to give here.

Fortunately, there were more intimate rooms where the couple would probably take most of their meals and enjoy having aperitifs and tea. The bedroom was curiously closed-in in a place where openness seemed appropriate. It was almost reminiscent of Flanders except for the mosquito nets positioned above the large bed.

"Well, my dear," said the Count, "we are here."

"Yes," noted the Countess, " and it's not forever."

At dinner the sound of drumming from the villages, so intriguing earlier in the day, startled them. The Countess stared at her husband with an expression just short of alarm. He gave her a smile of reassurance and raised his hand in a calming gesture. Ah, yes! The power of the drums. He had heard about that. The savagery, the superstition. The immensity of their sound. He would take all that on advisement. "We are in Africa!" he told his wife. "Let's enjoy it." She rose from the table and began to dance to the rhythm, flailing her hips and arms. They laughed together. The Count felt they would be all right.

The following day Monsignor Van Rolse, the colony's senior Catholic clergyman said a welcoming celebratory mass at the Boma cathedral. After the service Van Belle presented the Count and Countess to the Monsignor as well as to other notables: General LeMoine, the Commandant of the Force Publique, the colonial police force and army; the chief justice of the courts, Amadeo DeRossi; and an important plantation owner of the region, Hans Bogaerts, who acted as chief of what in Belgium would have been called a planters guild. The new arrivals also met a number of colonial officials, local shopkeepers, and settlers. These colonials regarded the Count and Countess as both their betters and their protectors.

Outside the cathedral the Count caught sight of a tall, bearded white man of dignified mien, perhaps fifty. He stood aside from the crowd. The Count had noticed this person inside the cathedral and recognized in the way he carried himself that he was not Belgian. He asked Van Belle about him.

"That's Reverend Parkins," said the aide. "English. Baptist Missionary Society. They have a station a bit to the east of here at Kimpese."

"Should I meet him?" asked the Count.

"If you like." The aide answered without enthusiasm. But he did not take the Count to meet the Englishman.

Greeting his well-wishers, the Count listened to the settlers' talk and tried to maintain his interest in it. But it soon occurred to him that contact with a non-Belgian might be beneficial, both socially and professionally.

During a lull in the greetings he broke away from Belgians and sought out the Baptist. "Welcome," he greeted the missionary in English, offering his hand.

"I should be welcoming you, Governor-General," said the man as they shook hands. He had alert eyes in a face that bore the lines of long experience in Africa. "I hope you enjoy your time in the Congo. I'm Larry Parkins." He invited the Count to visit his mission station at Kimpese.

"I mean to see some country once we get settled," said the Count. "Perhaps I can arrange a visit. You've been here a while, have you?"

"Long enough to get settled." The trace of a smile suggested British understatement. "The BMS has been in this region for fifty years."

The Count noticed Van Belle approaching, undoubtedly to fetch him. The aide said hello to the Baptist, then turned to the Count. "I'm afraid I must drag you away, sir," he said. "Please excuse us," he told Parkins.

"Glad to meet you," said the Count as he moved off. "We must talk sometime."

"I'll look forward to that," Parkins replied.

As they moved away, the Count asked, "Was that necessary?"

"Settlers are practically lined up to shake your hand," said Van Belle.

After greeting settlers, the Count and Countess shed their official roles and strolled through Boma. They moved past settler houses, rectangular structures with tile roofs. Behind them stretched clotheslines from which hung the white trousers, shirts, and dresses in which the settlers clothed themselves. Children played in the yards, some of which boasted lawns. Plants edged the yards. Their leaves - red, yellow, green, some striped and magnificent in size - seemed almost to glow. They gave the quarter its only exotic aspect. The neighborhoods stood in quiet orderliness as if seeking respectability. Settlers who recognized the Lippenses bowed gravely as they passed.

At the edge of the settler quarter lay a burial ground, surrounded by a low fence. "Shall we pay our respects?" suggested the Count. The couple entered and moved through the gravestones. He read names of men who came from what seemed every country of Europe. "So many died," he commented to his wife. "They came from everywhere."

"They died so young," said the Countess. "Some by their own hands. Reading these dates you want to weep."

The Count wondered if any of the young men they had met on the ship would spend eternity in graveyards like these which dotted the colony. He wondered if he would. Would his wife? He thought suddenly if anything happened to her, he would not know how to go on. "We must be careful of our health," he told his wife.

Beyond the settler quarter the couple came upon huts made of mud and wattle, formed out of tree stalks cut as high as a man, the roofs fashioned from banana fronds. Cloths stretched to dry over some of the same bushes the settlers used to decorate their plots. So close to the settler quarter men dressed like settlers in cotton pants and long-sleeved shirts. Women dressed African in bodices of patterned material, long cloths wrapped about their hips, some-times several cloths, all of them colorful in hues that did not match. Their heads bore elaborate cloths, often tied intricately.

Every woman, so it seemed to the Countess, had a baby or infant tied to her back. She noticed that small children acted as nannies to even smaller ones. As the Lippenses moved along, they enticed children out of the alleys behind the huts. Some wore shirts that barely covered their behinds; oth-ers danced about in threadbare shorts while still others were naked. The children moved as close to the newcomers as they dared, whispering among themselves. The Countess turned to watch, call greetings, and wave hellos to them, walking backwards and making them laugh. "Aren't they enchant-ing," she commented to the Count.

"Quite," he agreed.

What struck them most about the native quarter was the noise. It seemed to explode: drumming, laughter, yakking, the children dancing and giggling. Behind huts women, some naked to the waist, pounded manioc tubers in pestles, their legs spread far apart, their arms hurling mortars downward, shouting to friends as they worked. The Countess wondered what the men did. Then she saw a group of them, smoking pipes as they sat in shade and open air under roofs of banana or palm fronds.

"The men seem to enjoy their leisure," the Countess remarked.

"I'm sure they're discussing the fates of nations," said the Count.

When they saw the Governor-General and his lady, the men stood, bowed respectfully and stared. The half-naked women stopped pounding manioc and stared as well. "Those women were shouting to each other just now," observed the Countess.

"Announcing to friends that we were strolling through."

"It's rather fun, don't you think, to see the real Africa?"

"I'm told," said the Count, "it gets realer and realer the farther you get from Boma."

They turned back to the administrative quarter where they would live. A burst of yellow butterflies suddenly appeared. The Countess raised a hand hoping to catch one. They fluttered about her arm. "I'm glad we're here," she told her husband.

In that quarter above the estuary the Governor-General had an expansive office on the second story of the State House. Van Belle's office was adjacent, just outside it. Reports, correspondence, and visitors would all pass through Van Belle before reaching the Count.

Besides its desk, sofa and two easy chairs, the Count's office possessed two significant features. One was an enormous portrait, larger than life-size, the most immense portrait the Count had ever seen. From it a long-bearded King Leopold II gazed down with an expression which his admirers regarded as tenderness and his critics as profound self-satisfaction. When he first entered the office, the portrait startled the Count. He gulped. Would it always be staring down at him while he worked?

He knew that the settlers revered Leopold. They esteemed the political cunning by which he, the sovereign of a country hardly larger than a duchy, had persuaded other European powers to cede him the interior of Africa as his personal fief: the Congo Free State. Those kings and prime ministers mistakenly regarded the interior as impenetrable. If the king and his minions were rough in their management of that territory, the settlers admired their grit. After all, they knew how dense was the jungle, how blockheaded, superstitious, and violent were the natives, how swift was the great river, how enervating the climate.

The Count would not allow either the settlers nor the members of the colonial service to know that he regarded Leopold as a national embarrassment. He would keep personal feelings to himself. He understood that the palace in Brussels was watching him. There Leopold was venerated. And here in Boma he would be careful. He would not suggest that the portrait be removed.

The king's presence in the office would cause the Countess even greater distress. She found his private behavior deeply repugnant. She understood, of course, that monarchs were often paired with royals they neither loved or hardly knew. She realized that adventuresses hunted them and accepted dalliances. But she could not forgive the fact that at age sixty-five, even while his estranged queen lived, Leopold took as his mistress the sixteen-year-old French prostitute Caroline Lacroix. She had given him two illegitimate sons; at least it was said they were his. He lavished upon her estates, gifts, large sums of money and an inheritance that made her a multimillionaire. Five days before his death Leopold made Lacroix his wife. Seven months later she wed the man who had served as her procurer.

The Countess, too, would be careful to express this repugnance only to her husband. Her private narrative about how hers and her husband's experience in the Congo would unfold demanded discretion. Which meant rigorously keeping their opinions of Leopold to themselves. It required constant vigilance when burnishing their reputation with the palace in Brussels. The burnishing achieved, they would leave the Congo ripe for rewards. So if neither one of the Lippenses felt comfortable with the king's portrait staring at them, they would keep their own counsel.

The first time the Count saw the second significant feature of the office, he was not only startled. He jumped backwards. When his wife beheld it, she ran from the office. Van Belle said, "I'm afraid our friend embarrasses your wife. I almost removed him, but thought you should see him first." Van Belle seemed genuinely chagrined. "If I had known your wife was coming, I would have hidden our friend."

"We aren't here to hide from Africa," observed the Count. He studied the sculpture they were discussing. He said, "I think it may have as much right here as the sovereign." He glanced again at the portrait of the king and inwardly shuddered.

When the Countess peeked back into the room, she could not help laughing. "Darling," she said, "you cannot have this monster in your office."

"Why not? It will remind me of things I need to remember."

The sculpture was unmistakably a man – with a large head, a torso into which nails had been driven, and enormously tumescent masculine equipment.

"Then it must wear an apron." the Countess insisted. She shook her head, smiling at the size of his endowment. After a moment she asked her husband, "What can it possibly remind you of that isn't disgusting."

"African values," said the Count.

"Like what?"

The Count improvised. "A belief in spirits, the importance of reproductive capacity."

The Countess turned to Van Belle. "What is it anyway?"

"It's a nail fetish," he explained. "Some Kongo people believe that such a fetish can destroy evil spirits, prevent illness, thwart bad deeds." The Countess approached the fetish and inspected the rusty nails driven into its head and chest. "Occasionally the fetish must be provoked," continued Van Belle. "Hammering nails into it does the job."

"Did our predecessor consult it?"

"Occasionally he swore at it. But he never asked it for advice."

"If you are to keep it, my dearest," the Countess repeated, "it must wear an apron." She emphasized, "A very large apron."

"Can you see to that, Van Belle?"

The assistant nodded.

"As art," said the Countess, "it's quite stunning."

"I agree," said Van Belle. "But to them it isn't art at all. It's an actor from the spirit world."

"Must be a very lively world," observed the Count.

"If you ever pound nails into it," warned his wife, "I will insist we return to Belgium."

Later, as he sat alone in his office, the Count wondered exactly what he was supposed to accomplish as Governor-General. With the portrait staring at his back, he understood that he was to further the development of the colony. Industrially, that meant supporting and expanding the mining activity far to the east in the Katanga. The copper mines there were significantly enriching Belgium. It meant doing what he could for plantation agriculture. Socially, development meant winning the trust of European colonials that their interests were a matter of highest importance.

But as he regarded the fetish, about which Van Belle had now wrapped an apron, he wondered about the colony's Africans. He knew that he must rectify the outrageous Free State exploitation. African development would mean refining administrative structures, extending social services and retraining freebooters and adventurers to become administrators dedicated to the betterment of blacks.

It offered him the challenge of reforming the *chefferies*, the hundreds of chieftaincies across the colony in which the native population lived. But these were abstractions. How did he go about actually making progress? He thought for a moment of his shipboard companion Antoine Sambry who had come to the Congo to embrace his destiny. Soon he would be sent to the bush and given African troops to lead. The Count sensed that the Sambrys of the colonial service would have little appetite for "ruling to serve" or knowledge about "doing development."

What did development actually mean? Develop Africans toward what? Becoming ersatz Europeans? Missionaries, both Catholic and Protestant, were offering them, not only Christianity, but medical care and education, hoping to turn them into Christians. But education and medical care, though maybe not the Bible, would woo them away from their lives in the villages. So would work on plantations. Did plantation owners want Africans to become overseers? Did they want them to start competing plantations? Did missionaries expect converts to run their own churches? What about syncretism, the mixing of Christian ideas with those of African religion? Surely missionaries would object to that. But could political development actually be stopped? Wasn't that as impossible as holding back the tides?

The Count wondered if anyone had thought deeply about these matters and could offer answers. If such people existed, how could he identify them and learn what they thought?

FOUR

Even before the Governor-General settled into his office and his residence, visitors besieged him. They sought to capture his ear, to benefit him with their advice about the colony. To get ahead of them, Countess Lippens invited three men, met at the cathedral and designated as worth cultivating, to join her and her husband and Van Belle in the Governor-General's offices for tea.

Except in their desire to influence Count Lippens, the men were quite diverse. Monsignor Van Rolse, the colony's senior representative of the Catholic Church, was tall, imposing and in his mid-50s. He wore a white soutane, untouched by the messiness of Africa. From his jaw hung a long, gray beard, paying Leopold II the homage of imitation.

The Count sensed immediately that Van Rolse was a deft politician, expert at what the Church called upon him to do, which was to shepherd its interests in the colony. When the Monsignor entered his office, the Count noticed that he hesitated for the merest instant to nod toward the portrait, an obeisance to the king.

By contrast, Hans Bogaerts, the plantation owner, was a decade younger, virile, intelligent, and tanned, very much a man with his hands in the African soil. For his visit to the Governor-General he wore a white suit and white shoes, a sun helmet tucked under his arm. When he spoke or smiled, a large mustache danced on his upper lip. As the owner of plantations east of Boma, Bogaerts wanted the orderly and systematic agricultural development of the colony and policies that furthered the well-being of his workers.

The third guest, Amadeo DeRossi, the colony's highest judicial official, entered the Count's office behind the others, as if deferring to them both. He moved as noiselessly as a shadow, his hands held behind his back. As if to forge a bond with the Count, he praised the enormous portrait of King Leopold. "It's reassuring, I suppose," he said, "to have the leader always at your elbow."

"Indeed," replied the Count, choosing a word that signified nothing. "I wish I had a portrait like that in my chambers."

The Count wittily expressed his sorrow that he could not offer to send the portrait to him.

DeRossi laughed at this. He was short and slight with a small mouth and a very long nose. "Such a nose!" exclaimed the Countess after the guests had departed. "I mistook it for a sausage!"

The Count laughed. "A non-entity. A man who succeeds in a colony, but had no chance of success back home."

"What's his role here?" she asked.

"He provides a cover of legality for whatever the administration wishes to do. I intend to stay as far from him as possible."

The Count and Countess did not betray these private thoughts. While the guests were in their presence, they were exemplars of graciousness. Instead of tea, Countess Lippens offered them wine in a parlor off the offices. Van Belle poured it.

In their small talk the visitors learned that Count Lippens had no inkling, until the possibility was broached to him, that he might be a candidate for the Governor-Generalship. Serving quite happily in East Flanders, he knew little about the Congo. He invited his guests to talk about their experiences in the colony. The men reminisced and the Count was surprised to learn that the Portuguese maintained a flourishing colony in the area a couple of centuries before.

The Countess remarked, "We are overwhelmed at the quality of the countrymen we have met out here." Of course, it was flattery, but she spoke it with such seeming sincerity that this fact did not occur to the visitors.

"Not every Father is a saint," admitted the churchman, "although I wish the reverse were true."

"And yet," interjected Bogaerts with a grin, "every planter is a man of sterling character like myself! He treats his laborers with delicacy, yearns to pay the administration even more in taxes and never complains that there are too few white women in these parts."

Countess Joanna laughed, delighted by his wit. She wondered how many BaKongo mistresses the planter kept. And, for that matter, the Monsignor as well.

"Music to my ears," said Count Lippens. "It will be my pleasure to work with all of you."

"Unfortunately," remarked the planter, teasing DeRossi, "there are too many lawyers." The judge did not reply in kind. He only shrugged. "Wherever I've been," continued Bogaerts, "always too many lawyers."

The Count commented that he hoped to visit all parts of the colony although he did not wish to play Henry Morton Stanley who had famously explored the colony for the king. Bogaerts opined that a day on the river might be enough. DeRossi suggested that the Count read one of Stanley's books.

"It is worth knowing," observed the Monsignor, "that things often go wrong here for us just as they frequently did for Stanley. That the natives, for instance, are not always our friends."

"The Monsignor is being mischievous," said the planter. "He enjoys warning new arrivals that there are natives who would like to kill us all."

"My reading of recent history," observed the Count, "suggests that it is we who have done the killing."

Absolute silence greeted this remark. The Governor-General saw that he had significantly blundered. Bantering chitchat did not permit reference to such matters. The Countess looked alarmed. She noticed DeRossi and the Monsignor exchange a startled glance.

"The king could not have expected that," the Count added although he knew this was not true.

"More wine, anyone?" the Countess hastily asked. She gestured to Van Belle to refill the wine glasses.

"I wish I did not have to say it," commented Bogaerts, "but of the plantation natives I've worked with most are shiftless. They must constantly be urged to work. The barest few seem ready for any kind of supervisory responsibilities."

"I'm pleased to hear you speak of supervisory responsibilities," said the Count. "Because I've been wondering: Is it not the administration's obligation to raise our Congolese to a higher level? After all, we are the Belgian Congo now. No longer the Free State. We are not here simply to exploit blacks." The visitors shifted their weight uneasily.

"All in due time," counseled DeRossi. "Slowly does it."

"This place does have to pay for itself, you know," said the planter.

The Countess wondered what in the world her husband was doing. Discretion had been their byword.

But the Count persisted, "It may be indelicate to mention the fact that egregious exploitation was the charge leveled against King Leopold." The unease of the guests deepened. The Count saw he must retreat. He could not do this fast enough to satisfy the Countess. "Yes, he had vision and accomplished much good," continued the Count. "Still he was susceptible to charges of the worst kind of exploitation."

The Monsignor replied, "I never believed those charges, my dear Count. They were leveled against the king with an eye to nibbling up Free State territory."

"Enemies are always eager to take what we have worked so hard to secure," observed DeRossi. "The natives are only too eager to help them."

"My dear Count," said the planter, "don't let us misunderstand you. You don't really think that Leopold and all the stalwart men he gathered to bring civilization to this land of jungle and savagery—" He looked at the others, certain they all agreed with him. "That their motives were anything other than noble. The privations the Fathers endured! And for what reason? Only to bring Christianity to benighted natives. Surely, an amazing work of sacrifice and noble-mindedness."

"Thank you, my dear Bogaerts," said the Monsignor. "You have stated what needed to be said."

The Countess quickly broke in. "I assure you, gentlemen, my husband did not mean to cast aspersions on the great work of King Leopold. We Lippenses are utter admirers of him!" She smiled at each visitor and gestured Van Belle not to stint with the wine.

To his wife's chagrin, the Governor-General did not relent. "I only meant to emphasize," he declared, "that we of the administration must look to the future, to accomplishments that build on the work of the past. We must correct errors where they occurred and move forward with confidence."

The visitors glanced at one another. This Governor-General had much to learn about the realities of the colony, they thought.

Changing the subject, Bogaerts asked the Count if back in the metropole people in government were keeping an eye on an American of slave background, Marcus Garvey. He thought they should be. Garvey was trying to organize blacks throughout the New World.

The Count asked if black self-realization was not inevitable.

"Do you think so?" asked the churchman. "In my view the natives are manifestly unready for any kind of-- What did you call it? Self-realization? They're not ready for any kind of equality with Europeans."

"They hardly understand a legal system," observed the judge.

The Countess hastily said, "I'm sure Maurice did not mean that!" She laughed and shot her husband a scolding look to mind his tongue. "Thank God, Garvey's work is confined to the Americas," she exclaimed.

The Count watched this byplay, saying no more in order to mollify his wife. But he wondered what churchmen thought they were doing Christianizing Africans if it was not to ready them for some kind of self-realization. Did they suppose that converts would always be willing to follow the lead of priests? But hadn't that always been the Catholic expectation? Hadn't the Protestant revolution showed them the fallacy of that assumption?

Suddenly Bogaerts held up his hands, drawing attention to himself.

"Before I forget," he said, "I must tell you what I heard just before I left the plantation. The natives always surprise us, don't they?" He paused before he began his account. "It seems that in a village in the territory of Cataracts Sud a fellow passing through came upon a woman on her deathbed."

"Does this happen?" asked the Countess.

"She was lying on a pallet outside her hut, ready to die. Apparently the fellow once felt some kind of religious calling. Now it gripped him again. He went to the woman, laid his hands on her, and – this is interesting! – started trembling—"

"Trembling?" interrupted the Countess, intent on anchoring the conversation in new directions. She showed herself mildly astonished, somewhat skeptical, and rather amused. She glanced at her husband who seemed not to find it bizarre.

"Rumors suppose the Holy Spirit came upon him," explained Bogaerts.

"What happened?" asked the Countess.

"He raised the woman from her deathbed."

The Count felt a cold, inexplicable shudder sweep down his back. Would this event challenge the administration? He and Van Belle exchanged a glance.

Trying to keep the mood light, the Countess laughed. "That makes me tremble myself!" She began a mock trembling. The visitors smiled. But behind their smiles was a wariness of the report.

"Savages and the Holy Spirit!" the Countess exclaimed. "We don't believe such tales, do we?" The Count frowned at his wife. He felt she was as much out of line at this moment as she had felt him to be only moments before. She was allowing her guests to see her trying too hard at her party.

"It is never a matter of our believing the tales," replied the Monsignor. "But do the natives?"

"I'm afraid they do," said Bogaerts. As newcomers to Africa, the Count and Countess looked perplexed. "The rumors of this miracle – that's what the natives are calling it - spread like wildfire around my plantation."

"Precisely!" said the judge.

The Count turned to Van Belle. "What should we make of these rumors?"

"The question always is:" said Van Belle, "will they catch fire with the natives? If they do, there's no telling what could happen."

"Let's return to the terrace, gentlemen," suggested the Countess. "Talk of the Holy Spirit visiting Congolese: that quite spooks me. And exhausts me." She laughed brightly and hoped the visitors would leave. She knew her husband hoped the same thing.

Van Belle hurried to hold the door open as Countess Lippens led the three visitors onto the terrace. He saw that the Count did not intend to follow them immediately and remained behind.

The Count asked him. "What should we make of these rumors?"

Van Belle said, "The question is: will they catch fire?"

"They could be serious then?"

"If they catch fire."

"Let's find out if there's any credibility to them," Count Lippens instructed. "Who's our man in Cataracts Sud?"

Van Belle named the officer as Léon-Georges Morel, a young man in his late twenties, in the colonial service only about a year.

"*Merde!*" thought the Count. A man with hardly more experience in the colony than he himself possessed. Was it novices like the two of them who were responsible for running this vast colonial enterprise? He had supposed territorial administrators would be people like Van Belle.

"Morel seems capable," said Van Belle to reassure his superior. He added. "Of course, if this business blows up, he won't have had the experience to handle it."

"Find out everything you can," the Count directed, "and give me a report."

He and Van Belle hurried onto the terrace and down the entry stairway to bid *au revoir* to the visitors. As they left, Van Belle accompanied them.

The Count told his wife, "I'm going back to the office."

"I'll come with you." As they made their way there, the Countess asked, "How do you think that went?" The Governor-General grunted. "I did my best to cultivate that Monsignor."

"Be careful of him," remarked the Count. "Expects me to do whatever he advises. Not sure I like that."

When they entered the office, the Countess assumed a mischievous expression and sashayed over to King Leopold's portrait. She gave it an impertinent look and confided the latest intelligence, "The Monsignor intends to grow a beard even longer than yours, my dear sovereign. I wonder if he chases teenaged girls as you did."

The Count smiled – her sassiness had always charmed him – and put his finger to his lips.

"The planter was rustic with his rumors of a possessed savage." The Countess expected her husband to share her amusement, but saw that he winced at her last word. He refused to define his subjects by that term. His wife studied him. "You don't take that rumor seriously, do you?"

"Who knows what's 'serious' out here?" He added, "All that talk of 'natives.' The natives. The natives. Quite distressing."

"Promise me you won't try to change the way the settlers talk." The Countess regarded him carefully. "Are you all right, darling? You seem—" She did not finish her thought.

"I never had to deal with healers in East Flanders."

"Nor anything like this!" The Countess danced to the fetish and stroked his nails. She lifted the apron Van Belle had fixed on the sculpture and shook her head. "Amazing!" she said.

"I understand they come that way," the Governor-General said.

"Do they really?" She dropped the apron.

"Don't go investigating."

"I haven't much else to do."

"Give teas for the good wives of the settlers."

"How dreadful!" She looked again at the portrait, saluted it and squared back her shoulders. "We shall make ourselves proud."

"Yes. Let's!"

"But I warn you," she said. "Be careful what you say about dear old Leopold."

The Count smiled. "I frightened you for a moment, didn't I?"

"You did, indeed! I am trying to cultivate these men and you go running off at the mouth."

"We can't cultivate them if they think me a pushover."

"You are not a pushover. But you are a loyalist! A royalist. Here with the blessing of the palace." She added, "Don't forget: the palace is watching you."

"No, I won't," he promised. He returned to his desk and stood before it, staring at the correspondence and reports awaiting his attention. He could not refrain from remarking. "But we must not pretend that the Congo Free State was all roses and rainbows. Terrible atrocities occurred. Millions of Africans died."

The Countess moved toward him, her right hand extended. He took it. "Yes. But let's remember this, my dear: We are here first to make a brighter future for you." He shrugged. "Second, to shore up the colonial administration. Finally, if there are time and energies left, to make sure that the Belgian mining interests in the Katanga continue to flourish. All of that will keep you busy."

He smiled, amused by her combination of sassiness and cunning. "I wish you were handling this miracle worker," he told her. "It looks like the man we have for the job may not be up to it."

"That would be more interesting than giving teas." The Countess tapped him affectionately on the chest, "I will see you at dinner."

He watched her leave the room and sat down at his desk. He recalled the cold shudder that had swept down his back. He wondered what was the likelihood of "the business" blowing up. Fairly good, he imagined.

He thought: Transcendence must make an interesting change from daily life for Congolese. They were hustled into church and told what to believe, pushed into plantation labor and told what to do. The hustlers and the push-ers thought it inconceivable that Congolese should be interested in self-real-ization. But what were the trembling and the miracle healing if not attempts at that very thing? Of course, Congolese were seeking it. They were looking for one of their own to lead them out of the white man's religion and the white man's work. And the white man's government. After a moment the Count shifted in his chair to stare at the fetish. We have only just arrived, he thought. And already a miracle worker.

FIVE

N THE FREE STATE ERA LEOPOLD'S ADMINISTRATORS had divided the vast expanse of the colony into hundreds of *chefferies*, each of which was governed by an African *chefferie* headman. Some were traditional chiefs, already in place, administering their territories. Others, appointed, were Congolese known to administrators, former clerks or non-commissioned officers who had some familiarity with European ways, but lacked roots where they were expected to govern. Often such appointed chiefs were neither respected nor obeyed. The Ministry of Colonies feared that without urgent reform indigenous authority might completely collapse.

In the course of setting up the *chefferies*, an excessive number were established. Although "divide and conquer" principles were never acknowledged, they made establishing numerous *chefferies* an effective way of controlling territory.

Maurice Count Lippens' task was to eliminate excess *chefferies* and weed out ineffective chiefs.

It was a tricky reform, and it occupied his first months in the colony. Combining two or several *chefferies* into one unit made excellent sense on an administrative chart. But even combining two *chefferies* into one meant creating an excess chief. Each excess chief might regard himself as having a grievance against the colonial administration. Unless he could be cajoled, bought off, or somehow manipulated, he might cause trouble. It would be the job of the colony's territorial administrators to make excess chiefs accept the new system. That would require them to show tact, patience, and even fellow-feeling. These were not qualities for which Free State administrators were known.

The administration in Boma asked each territorial administrator to submit a plan for eliminating *chefferies* under his jurisdiction. The Count expected a good deal of slow-walking of the submissions. He realized that it would require tact, patience, and fellow-feeling from him and those instituting the reform to see it to achievement.

He did not need an African prophet who raised the dead to disturb the colony while he was trying to effect the reform.

Nor did he need another problem that came to his attention. Jean-Luc Baron Thibaud, a vice-Governor-General, resident at Kinshasa and charged with administering Congo-Kasai, a territory that stretched from the Atlantic well into the interior, made one of his periodic visits to Boma. Thibaud was tall, thin, with a craggy visage that some regarded as handsome. He had been in the colony for twenty years and would have been considered a candidate for Governor-General if the palace had not decided to try a new approach. After discussing a number of matters with the Count, he said rather reluctantly, "There's one final thing, totally under control, but I thought you would want to know about it." Thibaud paused, distressed that the matter might reflect badly on training on his watch, and plunged ahead.

"An attempt was made on the life of one of our assistant territorial administrators."

"That's a jolt," replied the Count. "Was our man badly hurt?"

"Not seriously injured, fortunately. A glancing blow by a knife. We patched him up."

"Who is he?"

"A man quite new to the service."

"Quite a welcome to Africa. And the attacker?"

"A Force Publique soldier stationed at the same post."

"Has he been caught? Arrested?"

"He fled into the bush. We're trying to track him down."

The Count pushed back in his chair to consider this news. He glanced at the nail fetish and imagined steam coming out of all those nails in his head as he ran at the officer, a knife glinting in his hand. An attack against an officer was serious business. A soldier killing an administrator could act like fire thrown into a tinderbox. Colonial control demanded that territorial administrators should seem invincible, as if protected by white man's witchcraft.

The Count was conscious that Thibaud studied him, trying to decide if he was up to the job. He rubbed his hand across his chin.

"Where is the officer now?" asked the Count. "In hospital?"

"He spent a day or two with his superior and returned to his post."

"What provoked the attack?

"Not entirely clear."

"No? What kind of investigations are your people doing?" Thibaud looked uncertain as to how to reply. "The soldier a bad egg?"

"The Force Publique people say no." After a moment Thibaud added, "There's a native woman involved."

"With our man?"

"Our man's story is that the soldier beat his woman. That's not unusual. Our man says she fled from the beating, fearing for her life. That is unusual. And, fearing for her life, she asked our man for protection."

"He knew her then?"

"He took her in. Protected her for a couple of days."

"Took in a soldier's woman? What the hell?"

"We think the soldier confronted our officer, less to do him harm than to retrieve his woman. If he lost her, he also lost his investment in her, the bridewealth he had paid for her." The Count frowned, not fully understanding. "Men buy their wives here," Thibaud explained. "He brought other soldiers with him. They dragged the woman away. Our man may have tried to protect her."

"Good Christ!" said the Count.

"That's when the soldier – Mbilo is his name - went after him. His mates pulled him away."

It was not difficult to see what the problem was here. "Did our man sleep with her?"

"He says not, but I'm afraid he may have!"

"Damn! Bloody hell! What kind of fool is he?" Then the Count asked, "Did he entice her into his quarters?"

"Our man says he did not? But Mbilo's buddies claim he beat the woman for flirting with a white man."

"Did our man have his eye on her?"

"Perhaps. He says not, but he'd been on post long enough. His fellows say Sambry has an—"

"Sambry!" exclaimed the Count. He leaned forward to glare at the Baron. "Sambry! Anatole? No-- Antoine! "

"You know him?"

The Count laughed ironically and shook his head. "We came out on the same ship. I met him there." He recalled the first time he encountered Sambry, he was making a play for the Countess. "Saw him lining up women for the trip. I confess I wondered what kind of an officer he'd make." After a moment he asked, "What does his superior think? He believe his story?"

"I doubt it. But we can't have soldiers attacking territorial administrators. Even if it's to get their women back."

"Sambry must have known that."

"I'm sure his superior assumed he did." Thibaud shrugged. "Our men will sleep with natives. Can't prohibit that."

"But, for God's sakes, not the women of soldiers under their command.

Do you have discipline options?"

"He can't stay at the same post."

"No. Have him transferred to another location. Have his superior read him out. And let him know that the transfer instructions came from Boma."

At lunch as he and his wife began their soup, the Count asked, "Do you remember that fellow Sambry?"

"Sambry?" she replied, teasing him, cocking her head as if searching her memory. "Sambry?"

"Don't play that game with me." His tone was both amused and impatient. "He gave you and half the females on that ship the bright eye."

The Countess laughed. "Bright eye? Is that what you call it?"

The Count put his soup spoon down. "He turned the same 'bright eye' on an African girl at his post. Her man happened to be a Force Publique soldier, a man named Mbilo."

"Billy!" exclaimed the Countess delightedly. "Let's call him Billy."

"If you like," said the Count. "Mbilo went after Sambry with a knife. Took some flesh off his bones.

"Goodness."

"Dangerous business for the administration."

They dipped into their soup again. The Countess hesitated, then asked, "Did Sambry—"

"The girl was in his house for two days so I think you can assume he did."

"Will you send him home?"

The Count held his soup spoon halfway to his mouth. "Transferred the damn fool to a new post and hope he's learned to keep away from soldiers' women." The Count drank from his spoon and added, "If he can't do that, he's in the wrong business."

"Flirtation," the Countess teased. "Being charming. That's his business." Then she asked, "What if he'd been killed?"

"It was hardly an attack. The man wanted his woman back Didn't want to lose the money he'd paid for her." He took another spoonful of soup. "He's being hunted now. They'll find him."

"And then?"

"Have a trial. Whip him with a chicotte probably. Execute him."

"You told Hugo you weren't coming out here to execute Congolese."

"The settlers will insist. So will the administration." He repeated the Baron's observation, "I'll try to prevent it, but we can't have black soldiers attacking white officers, even if the white man's a horse's ass."

"Maybe you should whip the horse's ass then. Sambry's endangering every white man, isn't he?"

"But he's white. The settlers would be furious."

They finished their soup in silence.

Because he could picture Sambry in his mind and on board ship had even taken a passing interest in him, the man's behavior irritated the Count. He wanted to tongue-lash the man. Before returning to the office, he paced around the residence garden, trying to walk off his annoyance. He realized he needed to talk to someone with experience of Africa. Someone who was not Belgian.

When the Count returned to the office, he asked Van Belle to see if Reverend Parkins, the English missionary to whom he had spoken at the welcoming mass, might be in town. If so, could Van Belle arrange a meeting?

This suggestion caught Van Belle completely off guard.

The Count smiled. "Your expression suggests that such an idea appalls you."

The assistant was not accustomed to such candor. It took him a moment to collect himself. He asked, "May I speak frankly?"

"Always," the Count assured him. "At least when we're alone."

Van Belle plunged ahead. "This is a Belgian colony, sir, and Reverend Parkins is English."

The Count did not want to get all his impressions of the Congo from Belgians, but preferred not to mention this fact to Van Belle. "Parkins has been here many years," said the Count. "Is that not reason enough--" Van Belle's discomfort made it unnecessary for the Count to finish his thought.

"Our supporters in Belgium," noted Van Belle, "both those well-connected and the common people, favor dissemination of the Catholic faith."

"And Reverend Parkins is Protestant."

Van Belle nodded.

"And since Belgium is a Catholic country, Catholics regard themselves as enjoying official favor." Van Belle stared at the floor like a schoolboy being chastened by the headmaster. "Didn't my inviting the Monsignor to be among my first guests signal that favor?"

Van Belle nodded again.

"Would my talking to a Baptist missionary set tongues wagging?"

Van Belle nodded yet again.

"Especially since it is already being noised about town that I described the Free State era in terms not recognized here as credible. Is that it?"

The aide straightened up and ventured a laugh. "I see that we are truly going to speak frankly to one another."

"I hope so," said the Count.

"I'm trying to give you the dimensions of how things work here."

"The Catholics will be watching what I do."

"And getting reports about it, I'm afraid," noted Van Belle. "You have met the Monsignor."

"Indeed I have. And by the way," the Count added, "I have a suggestion. Our guests the other day kept talking about 'natives.'"

"That's the lingo out here."

"Let's starting calling these people Africans or Congolese, shall we?" The Count noticed a flicker of panic pass across his assistant's eyes. "'Natives' sounds pejorative."

"Right, sir. Africans. Congolese."

The Count smiled to reassure Van Belle. "No fuss. Agreed?"

The assistant relaxed, even laughed slightly. "May I say, sir, you are quite a different Governor-General."

The Count shrugged, uncertain what this might mean. "Our Africans may like us better if we speak of them with respect."

"The settlers won't want to follow that suggestion."

"We won't try to change them."

"If the settlers can't denigrate the 'natives—'"

"Congolese," said the Count.

"I meant Congolese. They will be very unhappy."

The Count said simply, "We'll do what we can." He turned back to the matter at hand. "I would like to meet with Reverend Parkins if he's in town."

Parkins was pleased to meet with the Governor-General, so pleased, that the Count assumed his predecessors had paid scant attention to Protestant missionaries.

When they met in the Governor-General's office, the Count suggested, "Shall we speak English?"

"Please," said Reverend Parkins. "I've mastered it and several African languages, but French has always eluded me."

The Count watched Parkins appraise both the portrait of Leopold and the fetish in the corner. "I have these gentlemen with me in the office so that I can keep track of them."

Parkins gave a wry smile. "Villagers would regard them as fetishes, your spirit guides."

"I attempt to navigate between their worlds." The Count added, "Always a challenge to decorate an office."

Having just arrived, he said, there was so much he wondered about. Perhaps Reverend Parkins could share some wisdom. "I have years here," Parkins said, "I'm not sure they add up to wisdom."

The Count explained that he had recently received a report about an administrator involved with a Congolese woman. It led to problems across the color bar. "I don't imagine missionaries have such problems."

Parkins laughed. "I hasten to assure you, Governor-General, that missionaries are people." He explained. "Some of them come out here, not only men, where the local people are virtually naked, often showing very attractive bodies. It can be disturbing for our people."

"How do you handle things?"

"We fix their noses to the grindstone. They usually adjust."

"The woman who became involved with our young officer belonged to a Force Publique soldier," explained the Count. He briefly outlined the situation.

Parkins considered the matter. Finally he prophesied, "When they catch that soldier, the settlers will want him executed. Do you realize that?"

The Count did not reply.

"They'll exaggerate the attack and demand execution." Parkins looked seriously at Count Lippens. "How will you deal with that?"

My break-in challenge, thought the Count. He said, "I'll cross that bridge when I reach it."

Their conversation moved to other subjects. Acknowledging his own challenges in adjusting to Africa, the Count asked about how missionaries had managed to gain their first footholds in the region.

"It was very difficult," Parkins admitted. "Our people walked into unknown situations, bearing gifts for chiefs, of course, but never knowing if they were welcome. And so many of them perished." He mentioned a famous Baptist missionary of the previous generation who had lost his wife, then two brothers, a sister and a sister-in-law.

"Take care of yourself," Parkins advised. "We often work too hard out here. We expect to rebound from illness the way we would at home."

"We are being very careful already," the Count assured him. "We left our children in Belgium to be safe."

Parkins spoke of the first challenges the missionaries faced. They sought places to establish themselves, he said, but white people were suspect. Local people assumed all whites were freebooters, that they meant to take rather than to give. Parkins noted that the missionaries' real gift was a higher way of living, a more spiritual perspective of existence. "Our friend in the corner suggests the superstition we hope to replace."

Count Lippens turned to gaze at the fetish. "I like to think that my fellow countrymen came out here with some of the same intentions," he said. "But managing a colony turned out to be quite a challenge. I've wondered what can be done to improve the lives of Congolese."

The missionaries had puzzled over the same thing, Parkins said. They found that there was plenty of work to keep them busy: identifying local people who would welcome them as neighbors, establishing stations and the gardens that would feed them, beginning evangelizing work. "We've made a number of converts," said Parkins. "But Christianity's not easy for Congolese. Monogamy is regarded as a great burden. Relinquishing the spirit world is very hard. Witchcraft is deeply entrenched."

"How do you find converts?" the Count asked. He began leading to a matter he wanted to broach.

"Our original ones were boys that tribal enemies forced into slavery. They were rescued and brought to us. One or two have returned to their home territories to set up missions."

"I ask," the Count said, "because we've heard an interesting rumor." An African Christian was said to have raised a woman from the dead, he explained. Reports of the event had apparently created a stir. Parkins acknowledged that he had heard the rumor. Some people from Kimpese had gone to the man's village. "The healer may be a Baptist, one of ours," Parkins said.

"What should I make of this?" the Count inquired. "Do such healings really happen? Do rumors often float around?"

"Always something new out of Africa," Parkins noted. "Isn't that what they say? Every now and then there's someone who's deathly ill, but suddenly rises well from a sick bed."

"But I take it this recent business was seen as extraordinary," said the Count.

Parkins shrugged. "I can tell you," he said, "we've had our ups and downs fighting malaria and sleeping sickness. Some villagers contend our medicines cause blindness. They rather trust spirits and *féticheurs*. Or hammer a nail into that fellow lurking in the corner." Parkins regarded it, then observed, "The apron's a good idea."

Van Belle presented Count Lippens with the report he had requested, prepared by the young territorial administrator Léon-Georges Morel. It offered the opinion that the miraculous recovery of the woman waiting to die was fact, not rumor. Congolese were spreading word of the incident, calling it a "raising of the dead" and the healer "a prophet."

The healer was a MuKongo called Simon Kimbangu. Van Belle wrote out the name as Ki-Mba-Ngu, separating it into syllables to aid the Governor-General in pronouncing it. Kimbangu came from the village of Nkamba in the region of Thysville, the nearest town. He was of the BaKongo people and grew up in a family with deep Christian roots. His father had been a catechist, an itinerant teacher of the principles of Christianity. Both parents were now dead.

Informants described Kimbangu as having been an extraordinary child – Count Lippens wondered what that meant – full of wisdom and knowledge, a knowledge of a kind about which the Count was totally ignorant. Kimbangu had received baptism from the British Baptist Missionary Society in 1915, six years previously. For a time his uncle had served as an Anglican catechist. After the uncle's death Kimbangu took his uncle's widow as his wife. As a result of the woman's healing, Kimbangu, now in his early thirties, seemed to have begun a period of prophecy and healing.

Preaching and healing in his early thirties, Count Lippens thought. Where have we heard that before? An extraordinary child. "In favor with God and man," no doubt, thought the Count. Did all prophet stories possess the same elements? Or did self-proclaimed prophets tailor their stories to fit what missionaries taught? Whatever it was, the Count did not like the sound of it.

According to the report, some years earlier a vision had come to Simon Kimbangu. In it God called him to preach and heal. Instead of embracing the divine command, he fled. He feared the vision. Did it mean he was insane? His flight took him to Kinshasa, the largest town of the western Belgian Congo. There he worked as a domestic servant and at an oil refinery.

Now, said Moral's report, following the miraculous healing, hundreds of Congolese were flocking to Kimbangu's village.

Van Belle stood beside the Count's desk as he read the report. Once finished, Lippens asked, "Have there been other healers of this sort in this area?"

Van Belle said, "Two centuries ago a famous prophet arose in the old Kingdom of the Kongo."

The Count smiled ruefully. "This becomes increasingly unsettling. Who was he?"

"It was a woman," Van Belle continued. "Called Kimpa Vita. She began to preach. Not far from here actually."

"Is there something in the water?"

Van Belle smiled. "She healed. Won converts. Sent followers far and wide. If I remember correctly, she taught that Jesus, Mary and some of the saints were all black, born in the Kingdom of Kongo."

The Count tried to digest this information, wondering if Kimbangu – was that his name? Kim-Ban-Ngu? – would start preaching a similarly contagious doctrine. He asked, "How did authorities react?"

Van Belle said, "Kimpa Vita was captured by forces of the state. As I recall, she was tried as a witch and a heretic and burned at the stake." After a moment he went on, "Christianity is particularly susceptible to this kind of figure because Jesus promised to return, but has not done so." He paused. "As yet."

Count Lippens smiled, rose from his desk and began to move about the office. He asked, "It's not hard to see how this kind of thing unfolds, is it?"

Van Belle shook his head.

"Does this Kim-Ban-Ngu business involve the administration?"

"Not yet."

"Will it?"

"If it challenges the State."

"Has that happened?"

"Not yet."

"The extraordinary movement of people?"

"That will upset the settlers. They always fear that if the na— The Africans act in an organized way, it will be to kill them."

The Count stopped before a window overlooking the river and beheld the green vegetation beyond. He could envisage tremendous pressures being formed against the administration. He did not want his administration to get entangled with messianic movements or religio-political resistance cults or syncretist religion. Nor did he want his administration to face pressures to go hunting a prophet because settler groups feared he was a rebel. He did not want to face intimidation to put the prophet to death.

"Kimpa Vita was burned at the stake," the Count said. "Was her cult suppressed?"

"I believe so. The question always is: Once the cult acquires political goals, can those goals be exterminated? There's a pattern."

"Must the cult acquire political goals?"

"We are thirty-five hundred whites trying to govern millions of blacks. We make them work for us. We make them pay taxes. We force on them our religion. How can there not be a political dimension?"

The Count turned from the window. "I did not bargain for this when they asked me to become Governor-General."

Van Belle smiled ruefully.

The Count wondered if he had been a fool not to study more carefully the ramifications of the post when he'd been offered it. "You spoke of a pattern," he said. "What is it?"

"A prophet – or self-declared messiah - arises—"

"A real prophet or a resistance leader? Is this religion? Or politics?"

"Religion and politics fuse," Van Belle explained. "Prophets arise in situations like ours. Sometimes there is a perplexing complication."

"Which is?"

"The prophet turns out to be a man of true spirituality."

"*Mon Dieu!*" exclaimed the Count. "And it's part of the pattern that the state determines to crush the prophet?"

"Here's my theory," said Van Belle. "The prophet claims possession by spiritual forces. Healing occurs. Dispirited people become inspired. People who feel dispossessed by the elite suddenly become possessed by alternative possibilities. They call them spirits. But since the state knows only politics, it calls them rebels. The authorities feel threatened and act against what it perceives as a threat."

As the Count listened, a scene jumped into his mind. A white man with the best of intentions, perhaps the Governor-General himself, moved through the bush. He walked carefully, trying to make no false steps. Suddenly a lion rushed out of a bush to devour him.

The Count shook the image from his mind. To relocate himself in his office he stared intently at Van Belle. His train of thought returned. He asked, "Is this genuine healing?"

"Yes. But the prophet may not be a healer."

The Count frowned. What did this mean? A lion was charging him and his assistant talked in riddles.

Van Belle explained. "The healer gives the patient a new view of possibilities. For example, that blacks can heal themselves. The new view does the healing."

"How can that be?" asked the Count.

"The common people realize that their identity does not need to be determined by the ruling elite. The new view frees them from humiliation. They feel rejuvenated, expectant, emboldened. And they're healed."

"The prophet transforms their view of themselves?"

"Something like that." Van Belle shrugged. "The Congolese look at the matter somewhat differently. I don't mean politically. They regard Kimbangu as the Second Coming of Christ."

The Count stared at Van Belle, astonished.

"That designation has tremendous power," the assistant pointed out. "Even if Kimbangu doesn't claim it. Which he doesn't."

The Count frowned, not understanding.

Van Belle explained. "The missionaries – particularly the Protestants – tell the Congolese that Christ promised to return. It hasn't happened yet, but could happen any day. Then Kimbangu starts to heal. The Congolese ask themselves: Why not here? Why not now?"

Count Lippens returned to his desk and began to make notes on a tablet. Finally he asked, "Can we channel this in a positive direction? If this is religious, must we respond?"

"How to respond: that is always the challenge for authority."

The Count remained in his office the rest of the afternoon. Van Belle heard him pacing back and forth virtually the entire time. On the few occasions when he stopped pacing, Van Belle wondered which he was consulting: the king's portrait or the fetish.

The Governor General was uncommunicative when he had a glass of wine before dinner with the Countess. She asked what was troubling him. He introduced her to Simon Kimbangu, pronounced Ki-Mba-Ngu. The name made her laugh. She was tempted to make remarks, but saw that her husband was concerned. Remarks would only annoy him. He told her about the well-intentioned white man moving through the bush, only to be charged by a lion. The Countess touched his arm supportively.

"Kimbangu heard voices," the Count told her. "Didn't Joan of Arc hear voices?"

"I believe she did."

The Count rose and paced around the room, holding the wine glass in his hand. The lion was pacing inside his head. "Joan of Arc," he said. "St. Paul. Any number of saints. They all heard voices." He seemed almost to be muttering to himself. He shot his wife a glance. "What about St. Joan's voices?"

"Didn't they tell her to drive the English out of France?" the Countess replied. "The British caught her and burned her at the stake." The Countess allowed herself a saucy smile. "She died a virgin. What a waste!"

They both guffawed. "Must you?" asked her husband.

The lion disappeared in a puff of smoke.

At dinner the Countess asked, "Must the state get involved? Isn't this a religious matter?"

"Exactly what I've been wondering."

"Keep clear of it if you can, darling. Could it get out of hand?"

"Yes. I did not come here to deal with prophets!"

The next morning the Count received a telephone call from Baron Thibaud in Kinshasa. He let the Governor-General know that Mbilo, the Force Publique soldier who had attacked Sambry, had been captured, arrested, jailed, and was awaiting trial. The Count asked to be kept informed. At lunch he told his wife that "Billy" had been found.

Later, when the Governor General quizzed his assistant about Kimpa Vita, he learned that she professed to be a Christian and was said to preach from the Bible. He inquired if Van Belle knew anything about the Bible. The assistant acknowledged that he knew a bit. The Count said that long ago his mother, very devout, had told him Bible stories. "Are you religious?" asked the Count. "I'm not."

Van Belle shrugged and finally admitted that he had studied for the priesthood. The Count found that interesting. Van Belle hastily assured him, "But only briefly."

"Why did you give it up?"

Van Belle looked sheepish. "I learned about love."

"Before your vow of celibacy took effect?"

Van Belle smiled embarrassedly.

"And when it came time to take the vow--"

Van Belle shrugged again.

The Count laughed heartily. "Thank God for sin in the world!" After a moment he asked, "In your studies: Do you remember exactly what Christ said about coming back?"

"'Tarry till I come.' They expected him to return soon."

"Did he say, 'I will come back here?'"

"People in those days had little conception of traveling very far."

"Was it, 'I'll come back only once?' Or is that merely Second Coming tradition?"

"They expected his reappearance to signal the end of days. The end of time. Of the world."

The Count asked, "Is there a Bible around anywhere?"

Van Belle went to find a Bible. While he was gone, Count Lippens looked at the portrait and said, "I'm sure you don't have one, Your Majesty." He turned to the fetish, "How about you?"

When Van Belle returned with a Bible, the Count asked, "Where do I find the conversion of St. Paul?"

"Book of Acts. Well in."

"He heard voices, right? Where did that happen?"

Van Belle quickly withdrew as if to distance himself from any task of biblical interpretation. The Count investigated the Bible for several hours, sometimes reading on the couch, other times at his desk.

That evening before dinner as the Count and his wife sipped aperitifs, he reported, "I studied the Bible today."

"Has Africa driven you to that?" she asked.

"Interesting book," observed the Count. "Words to live by." They laughed together.

The Count was grateful for this time of relaxation. His feet lay on a hassock. His back nestled into his chair. His hand lightly held a potion that would soothe him. But what truly refreshed him was the chance to speak of his work with his wife who tended to regard the colony as a kind of satire. That helped him refresh his perspective.

"I have a project for you," he told her. "Would you be willing to undertake it for the greater glory of Belgium?"

"Phrased that way how can I refuse?" She asked, "What kind of project?"

"Research."

The Countess sipped her aperitif. "You need a university graduate for that. Not me."

"You're precisely what I need."

"Is it spying?"

"If it's spying, does it interest you?" The Countess smiled. "I need you to compile a dossier on a mysterious lady. She was called Kimpa Vita."

"A Mata Hari?"

"A woman much more fascinating." The Count explained that information about Kimpa Vita would help him understand how an earlier government had dealt with a prophet. The Countess agreed to the project, intrigued. It sounded much preferable to her than giving teas for settlers' wives.

SIX

Hardly had the Count settled down at his desk to read reports from the various provinces when Van Belle entered to say that Monsignor Van Rolse, who seemed to have arrived running, wished to see him. The Count was not surprised. Morel's report about Simon Kimbangu had obviously reached the Monsignor, provoking his appearance. The Count nodded that his visitor should enter.

"My dear Monsignor, welcome," greeted the Count.

The churchman seemed almost out of breath as if he had truly run to the Governor-General's office. "Thank you for seeing me," he said. "I heard the news. We must handle the matter of this man Kimbangu. It's urgent."

"Interesting that you should call," said the Count. "I was reading the Bible yesterday."

With a sly smile the Monsignor opined, "No good can come from that." He took a seat on the opposite side of the Count's desk. "Whenever people tell me that, I know I'm in for a rough ride."

Before the Monsignor broached the reason for his visit, he said, "By the way, I think you should be careful about consulting Protestants. The endeavor we're embarked on is Belgian. It carries the name *Belgian* Congo. British Protestants may not share our interests."

The Count was not surprised that Van Rolse knew of his meeting with Reverend Parkins. He accepted the Monsignor's advice without replying. He was damned if he'd allow the churchman to tell him how to do his job. However, he did permit him to offer lengthy counsel about the dangers Kimbangu posed to the entire colony. He also suggested possible ways for the authorities to deal with those dangers.

Shifting subjects, the Count asked, "What do you think happened to Moses on Mount Sinai?"

"Goodness!" remarked the churchman. "You have been reading your Bible." He put his left hand to his chin, the index finger resting on his lips, and considered the question. Finally he said, "Something that could not possibly happen today. Our ways of life are too different."

"When he came down from the mountain," the Count said, "his face shone like the sun. His people could not look at him until he covered his face with a veil."

Van Rolse nodded at this comment, but said nothing. He would not be drawn on what had happened and what it meant.

"Rods into snakes," said the Count. "The leprous hand. The burning bush. Was that all mesmerism?"

"Mesmerism is an interesting speculation," acknowledged the Monsignor. "I'll mull that."

"Paul on the road to Damascus: What happened?"

"To be frank with you, Count, I have often asked myself that very question." The Monsignor observed the Count with concern. There were times for biblical musings; he would be the first to acknowledge that. But this was not that time. He felt certain that Count Lippens was out of his depth. Why did the palace send out governors-general who had no experience of Africa?

"A light from heaven shone and a voice spoke to Saul, as he was then known. Was he insane, even momentarily?"

"Probably not."

"A voice spoke to him. The men with him heard the voice."

"And were astonished."

"Who spoke to him?" The Monsignor shrugged. "And on the Mount of Transfiguration."

The churchman shifted uneasily in his chair. "I know where this is going, my dear Governor-General," he said. "I am not going there."

"Paul said it was Jesus," stated the Count. "Who was dead. And resurrected and later ascended, some say. Could the dead – or the ascended – Jesus have actually talked to Paul?" The churchman raised his eyebrows, but made no reply. "Later Paul had to escape from Damascus in a basket," the Count continued. "The authorities – us! - were after him." Van Rolse said nothing. The Count went on, "Paul did a great work for Christianity. And for the world. Must we not assume that the authorities were wrong?"

"As I say," explained the Monsignor, "I am not going there."

The Count continued relentlessly. "God speaks to Jesus, Moses, Paul, Jonah (who runs away)—"

"And to the criminally insane. I have heard the confessions of criminals who told me God spoke to them."

"But the insane do not heal the sick."

The Monsignor shrugged. "You know your Bible well."

"My good mother's training. God spoke to little Samuel who was just a child."

Van Rolse looked annoyed, irritated, tired of this discussion. "But not to our natives." He raised the index finger of his hand and waved it back and forth.

"Why not?"

"Because our natives are savages," the Monsignor declared with conviction. "Kimbangu's people claim he's the Second Coming. What outrageous blasphemy!" The churchman leaned forward and shook his fist. "There are places where blasphemy is punished by death. I wish it were so here."

The Count shook his head. "Monsignor," he asked, "how could Kimbangu be a savage? He's a Christian! His father was a catechist. As he was himself. Kimbangu claims that God talks to him. If He does, should we interfere?"

"My friend, you have been here only a few months. Let those of us with experience guide you in this."

"And how would you propose I do this?"

"Show some humility, my son." It annoyed the Count to have the churchman-politician refer to him in this way, but he had long training in masking such annoyance. "Let us lead you." The Count nodded for him to continue.

"I talk with God every day," claimed the Monsignor. "When I do, I listen carefully to what He tells me. He reminds me that there is one true church and that I am its representative in the Congo. My task is to resist whatever would undermine the one true church in this place. That is why this Kimbangu must be stopped." He changed course, attacked from a different front. "Do you pray?"

It was the Count's turn to shrug.

"Start praying regularly, my son," the Monsignor advised. "And listen well. You will be told that you represent the order and stability that Belgium is trying to establish in this place of savagery. Of the illumination it is trying to set alight in this land of darkness. Your responsibility is to thwart all those who seek to undermine that order." The churchman leaned across the desk and touched the Count's hand. The Count forced himself not to withdraw it. "It is a high calling. You must not back away from it."

The Count sat back, escaping the touch of the church. "During his blindness Paul must have realized that it was untenable to keep killing believers of this new prophet," he said, returning to the earlier discussion. "And so it is with us. We can't kill or jail or rusticate everyone who sees things differently than we do."

Van Rolse patiently shook his head. "No, not as individuals," he agreed, "we can't do that. But as Governor-General it may be necessary. Your job is to maintain order and stability. You do not act as an individual. The status quo must be protected. That is my job. That is your job."

"I will 'think on these things,'" said the Count. "Perhaps that is enough wisdom for today."

"The wisdom for today," rebutted the Monsignor, "is this: 'While you have the chance, squash this bug.'" He shook the Count's hand and departed.

In the afternoon the Count received a telephone call from Baron Thibaud in Kinshasa. He reported that the Force Publique soldier Mbilo who had attacked the administrator Sambry had stood trial. The territorial administrator acting as judge had sentenced him to execution, after whipping by chicotte, the rhino hide whip.

Count Lippens instructed the Baron that no execution was to take place until he authorized it. The Baron expressed surprise that the Count wanted to involve himself in such matters. The Count told him, "At least until I'm confident in what I'm doing here, I want to be involved."

Van Belle remained in the Governor-General's office during the telephone call with Baron Thibaud, his hands clasped behind his back as he stared at the floor, his expression drawn. The Count returned the receiver to its cradle and noticed his assistant's attitude. "I must be getting better at reading your thoughts," he told his assistant. "I take it you disagree with what I've done." Van Belle shifted his weight, shrugged, spread out his hands as if to speak, but remained silent. "We agreed to speak frankly to one another. Don't stay silent."

Finally Van Belle said, "In the past I have not intervened in these affairs."

"And you think that's wise."

"The colony has several hundred territorial administrators, sir, and many of them are doing things a lot worse to blacks than competing with them for women."

"I have no trouble believing that. But how does it justify executing a Congolese?"

"We have limited powers. And we are few. So our control must be firm."

"Sambry started this kerfuffle."

"But our safety requires that natives must not attack whites." He paused. "I mean Congolese."

The Count smiled. "No, you mean natives."

Van Belle felt emboldened. "Yes, I do mean that. And sometimes one man must be punished harshly to make the point for all men." He excused himself and started for the door. But before leaving, he asked, "Are you considering commuting the sentence?"

"Possibly."

"There may be repercussions. The settlers feel safer if the administration is hard. They want firm control."

"Thank you. I'll cogitate."

Van Belle withdrew, leaving the Count to pace about the office, wondering what to do.

At lunch the Count broke the news to his wife. "The administration has sentenced your friend Mbilo to death."

"That's an outrage. You won't permit it, will you?"

The Count laughed and felt a weight lift off his shoulders. "What a joy to talk with someone with a capacity for outrage!"

"You won't permit it, will you?" the Countess repeated.

"Van Belle thinks I shouldn't intervene."

"Fire him!"

The Count laughed again.

Clouds gathered over Boma while Count Lippens and his wife had lunch. Returning to the office, he noticed that the clouds grew thicker, deeply black. Eventually rain began to fall, lightly at first, then heavily. The individual drops became thick as a curtain. When the Count stood observing the rain from his window, he could not discern the river below.

Watching the rain, the Count mulled an action he had considered for some days. Eventually he called Van Belle to join him.

When the assistant entered, the Count nodded for him to close the door. "What rain, eh?" said the Count. "Sit down. Why don't you?"

Van Belle rarely sat in the office and so this request – it seemed almost a social invitation, as if for a chat – rather surprised him. He took a chair. Looking up, he saw that the Count was studying him.

"I hope you will not think me presumptuous," continued the Count, "if I invite you to talk about yourself."

The assistant felt immediately on edge. "Pardon, sir?" he asked for this "invitation," as the Count called it, was unprecedented. The two men watched each other.

"Thinking about the advice you gave me this morning, I realize I know nothing about you. Except that you are vital to me. So tell me about yourself."

This request flustered Van Belle although he saw that it was reasonable.

"You've been here for ten years, is that right?"

Van Belle adjusted himself to reinforce the persona he showed to the world. He shrugged boyishly and said, "Why did I come to this place? Is that it? We've never discussed that, have we?" Why had he come: that was the usual question. He tried to relax. "The usual reason, I suppose."

"Which is?" The Count smiled.

"I wanted out of Belgium. It seemed too small. I wanted more than it could give me." Again a shrug. "I wanted to see the world." Van Belle looked at the nail fetish standing in the corner of the office. The Count followed his gaze. "Perhaps I had seen things like that and wanted to know more about them."

The Count looked back at his assistant in a quiet, patient way, and Van Belle knew that he would not be satisfied with the persona he usually showed the world.

"Within our first week in Boma, we had some gentlemen here for afternoon drinks," said the Count. "My wife asked you to serve wine."

"I remember, sir."

"You did it perfectly at ease, as if you were *de la maison*. I was impressed." Van Belle nodded his thanks for this approval.

"You've had some social training." Van Belle nodded again. "Most young men who come out here are lacking that," observed the Count. "If our friend Sambry had had some social training, he would never have made the mess he's caused."

Van Belle considered that remark for a moment, then said, "I'm the son of a doctor. From a medium-sized Flemish town. Social training was something I got growing up."

Again the two men watched each other.

The Count said, "You tell me that you studied for the priesthood. That's what makes me realize that I know nothing about you." The two men regarded one another. "Other, of course, than that you are the perfect assistant, of invaluable help to me, immensely capable, appropriately self-effacing. But I feel I should know you. Am I being presumptuous?"

Van Belle smiled, relieved by the praise, but still on edge. "Of course not."

"How did you happen to come to this wild place?" The sound of the question reverberated amid the rumble of the rain outside. "Most of the men who come here bring a certain wildness with them. Either they have it in them like Sambry or they're looking for it. Not surprising that such men got the Free State into a lot of trouble. But you are clearly not that sort of person. You've had some university?"

"Yes."

"But you didn't finish." The Count hoped that what he wanted to be a chat would not seem to Van Belle an inquisition. Van Belle shifted his gaze away from the Count who asked again, "Am I being presumptuous?"

Van Belle shrugged and shook his head, "No." Then added, "No, I didn't graduate." And finally said, "I came here because I had to get out of Belgium."

The Count watched the rain. He could not remember rainfall of such heaviness and thickness in Flanders. "Tell me more."

Van Belle sat very quietly, looking at his hands.

"This is meant to be a chat," said the Count. "And we're both feeling uncomfortable. I don't want to question you."

"I'm not used to talking about myself."

Without speaking, the Count smiled, trying to appear like a somewhat older colleague, not like a Governor-General.

"I had to get out of Belgium. But where could I go? This seemed the obvious place. I could find a job. I could be among Belgians."

The Count nodded, watching his assistant, waiting for more.

"I took passage on a boat. It brought me here. I got off and applied for a job with the administration."

"You were clearly a cut or two above the usual applicants and we took you." The Count still watched. Then said, "And the rest is history. Is that it?"

"I came to know the right people, both settlers and natives – Congolese - which is what my father would have told me to do. Absorbed what I learned and stayed out of trouble."

"Why study for the priesthood? That seems—" The Count shrugged.

"I was bored at university. It was preparing me for law, business. I didn't want that," Van Belle said. "I wanted to make a difference in the world." He smiled, a little sheepishly. This admission seemed to embarrass him.

"You've done that here, haven't you?"

"Have I?" He opened his hands doubtfully. "That's what a fellow wants in his early twenties: to make a difference."

"Yes, that's what I wanted," agreed the Count. "Then the war came along. I sat in a German prison camp for several years." Then after a moment he added, "But that didn't drive me to the church."

"The priesthood seemed designed to do that. But maybe. . ."

"You said you learned about love."

"I guess I thought I could do without that."

"Not easy for most men."

"I came to it late." Van Belle looked at the Count almost accusingly. "Are you going to ask me what that was about?"

The Count smiled understandingly, neither asking nor denying that he would ask.

Van Belle shifted in his chair, wondering how he could escape this interview, but knowing he couldn't. He wondered, too, if the Count and Countess speculated about him over dinner. He asked, "This is confidential, isn't it?"

"Of course," the Count reassured him. "This entire conversation is confidential."

Van Belle hesitated. If he means to hear the story, he thought, I might as well tell it. "I fell in love with a married woman," he said. "'Desperately in love' is how cheap novels describe it."

"But it wasn't cheap."

"No. It was exalting. She was a longtime friend. Her husband was away on a trip for several months. I saw them both often. When he was away, her smiles began to have an element in them that they'd never had before. I couldn't stay away. I'd never felt an attraction so strong for a woman and suddenly we became lovers. We—I'd never felt anything like that."

The Count said nothing, waiting for more.

Van Belle shrugged. "I felt terrible guilt. We both did. She loved her husband. She loved me. And I was studying for the priesthood."

"Quite a mixed-up time for you," observed the Count.

Van Belle laughed. "Yes. When her husband was about to return-- I couldn't be with her in his presence." He halted his story, looked at the floor. Then as if deciding there was nothing to lose in telling, he continued. "He was my brother."

Ah ha! thought the Count. That answered a lot of questions.

"He would see immediately—" Van Belle did not finish the thought. The room fell silent except for the sound of rain.

The Count smiled like a friend. "You took a ship to the Congo."

"It turned out that someone with my background had a future here," Van Belle said. "I didn't even have to leave Boma."

"Have you been here the whole time?"

"No. I had a job in a mining company for a time in Katanga."

"Is that a place I ought to visit?" asked the Count. He knew that the mining operations there provided the bulk of the colony's wealth and wondered if he should take a look.

"Quite a trek to get there."

"Did you take to mining?" Presumably Van Belle had not taken to it, for he had returned to Boma. The Count was merely encouraging him to tell more about himself.

"It was a much better fit for me in the administration." More silence. The Count kept waiting. Van Belle avoided his eyes. He realized he might as well tell the whole story. "I married a woman there, a mining engineer's daughter. In about the first month we knew it was a mistake." He lifted his shoulders. "I might have liked mining better if it had worked. But it didn't." He shifted in his chair. "After three years she went to South Africa. I returned here."

Unlucky in love, thought the Count. Not that there were a lot of women to choose from in the colony. Still, he must have seemed a catch. He wondered if Van Belle were still carrying a torch for his brother's wife in Belgium. "The administration was fortunate to have you return," observed the Count.

"It was trying to undo the worst of the Free State," said the assistant. "I realized that if I wanted to make a difference in the world—" He shrugged again for that seemed very much a young man's goal, not something he should espouse in his mid-thirties. "I guess there was still some of that."

"Worn away by now?"

"Mostly. I've made my peace with the world." He smiled modestly. "And with fellows like that." He gestured once again to the nail fetish. "I decided to get to know the people and their history and their language. Which I've done."

"Invaluable for us," said the Count, realizing how completely he relied on Van Belle for the knowledge he carried around inside his head. "How did you learn the language? Do you have a knack for that?"

Van Belle hesitated, but perhaps it was just as well to tell. "I found a patient young Kongo woman who'd had some mission schooling and had talent as a teacher. After a time I hired her as my house servant. She cleans the house, does the laundry, cooks and continues to teach me both the local language and Lingala." After a moment Van Belle added, "She lives in – she has her own room - because my house offers her much better living than a hut in the village."

"A useful arrangement."

Van Belle nodded agreement.

The rain was lessening. The Count rose from his desk and went to the window. He could see the river again through what was now light rain. Van Belle joined him at the window. "I guess we have survived the rain," remarked the Count. "Did you ever see rain like that in Flanders?"

"I should get back to work," said Van Belle. He left the office.

The Count watched the rain as it gradually stopped. He assumed Van Belle slept with his language instructor-servant. It was an excellent way to learn local languages, local mores. Maybe he had become lucky in love at last.

As they had aperitifs together before dinner, the Count told his wife, "During that rain this afternoon I got Van Belle talking about himself."

This news interested the Countess. Because they knew so little about him she had sometimes referred to the man as The Mysterious Monsieur V.B. "Well, well," she said. "What did you learn?"

The Count gave her a summary of their talk. Then he added, "He studied for the priesthood. Left for what I suppose is 'the usual reason.'"

"Who was she?"

The Count would not tell his wife as much as Van Belle had told him. "A married woman," he said. She did not need to know that he had been betraying his brother. "I take it he hadn't had much prior experience. He must have been surprised to find himself making love to another man's wife while studying for the priesthood."

The Countess raised a wicked eyebrow. "Isn't that part of the instruction these days?" The Count laughed. "Everything a young priest should know in order to serve his parish."

The Count mentioned that Van Belle had worked in Katanga for a time, that he had found administration more to his liking, more suited to his talents, than mining. "Married a settler's daughter out there. Only lasted a few years."

"I should think settlers' daughters would have their eyes on him here in Boma."

The Count said he had not inquired about that. It seemed awkward enough to call him into the office and suggest he recite his background. The chat had been cordial, however. The Count did not mention to his wife the live-in language instructor-servant. If he did, she would make the same assumptions he did, but react to them differently. To a man it seemed perfectly natural that Van Belle should find a woman for his bed, even if she were an African. His wife, however, might think less of him. He considered Van Belle an excellent assistant and did not want his wife thinking ill of him.

When they met again the next morning, the Count felt a greater warmth between them. Not a friendship certainly, but a basis for trust. "My friend," said the Count, "I am afraid I'm going to disappoint you."

"I doubt that, sir."

"I'm commuting the death sentence on that soldier to ten years in prison. Can you prepare me a letter about that for Baron Thibaud? And I'll sign it."

SEVEN

ONE EVENING BEFORE DINNER AS THE COUNT and his wife sipped aperitifs, he reported, "The Monsignor is visiting me tomorrow."

"Dreadful man," she commented. "Full of ideas about how to run your colony?"

"*His* colony as I believe he sees it. After all, we governors come and go. He stays." He continued, "Dreadful man, indeed. When I last saw him, he counseled me to 'squash the bug,' meaning this prophet that's arisen."

"Let's squash him," suggested the Countess.

"Let's have dinner," countered the Count, "and forbid the mention of his name."

The next morning Van Belle entered the Governor-General's office to announce, "Monsignor Van Rolse is here." The Count groaned in his head. But he understood that he must not antagonize a person who could give him much help or do him much harm.

"Give me five minutes," instructed the Count, "then send him in."

He used the five minutes to clear his desk and, more importantly, to review what had been said at the earlier meeting.

When Van Rolse entered, he strode forward with great purpose and offered his hand across the desk. "My dear Count," he said, "I beg your indulgence. I hope I am not becoming a nuisance."

"Nonsense," replied the Count, "It is always a pleasure to see you. Thank you for giving my wife the monograph about Kimpa Vita. I am trying to get up to speed."

"That is wise," replied the Monsignor, "because things are moving very quickly." The churchman pulled one of the lounge chairs close to the Governor-General's desk, sat down, and leaned forward so purposefully that the Count feared he intend to crawl across it. "I've come because I fear that you may not be getting sufficiently urgent counsel from the people advising you. Or that, because you have arrived here so recently, you are not yet able to interpret it accurately."

"My impression is—"

"This Kimbangu business is more alarming than you think," insisted the Monsignor, interrupting the Count. "It is spreading much more quickly than when I was last here."

The Count endeavored to speak, but the churchman overrode him. He warned that a mass movement was already forming. The bush telegraph, the talking drums, was broadcasting the news for miles. He reminded the Governor-General that workers were deserting plantations. The nearby churches were empty. The superstitious crowded all roads leading to Nkamba. He predicted that other prophets would pop up, as they always did. "The way to handle this," he declared, "is to snuff it out before it spreads."

"You left me with that counsel when we last met," said the Count. "I assure you I gave it much thought. If I may speak frankly, it staggered me."

"Then let me 'stagger' you again," implored the churchman. "Send someone to Kimbangu's village. Arrest him. Imprison him."

The Count watched with wonder as the Monsignor gave him advice more appropriate to the commander of the Force Publique.

"If necessary," he insisted, "execute him."

The Count did not mention that he had just commuted the sentence of a man condemned to death. With some astonishment he asked, "Execute a healer?"

"You don't want this to get out ahead of you. That can happen very quickly."

"On what charges would I have him arrested?"

"Sedition."

"For healing people? A man of God gives me this advice?"

The Monsignor rose from his chair to stand above the Governor-General. "The man claims that God talks to him. Don't you see the power of that? What if the natives believe him?"

The Count left his chair and came from behind his desk. "But what if it's true?"

As if he were protecting himself, the churchman's hand flew involuntarily to his chest. "You shock me, my dear count," he declared. "It is not true. Yes, we tell them that when we pray God speaks to us. And that He speaks to them, but only through us. They believe us because they see our material wealth, our education, our medicine. We say these come from our God." He looked at the Count imploringly. "If they begin to believe that God speaks directly to them, who knows what will happen?"

The Count held up his hands to slow this outpouring of excitement. Brought about by a dislike of the Monsignor, he asked, "But what if Kimbangu manifests the Second Coming?"

Now it was the Monsignor who was astonished. "Shall I tell the palace that you ask such a question?"

"Yes. And tell the Vatican as well."

"Does the King know of your lunacy?"

The Count moved back behind his desk. "My dear Monsignor," he said, "I am merely suggesting that we look at the matter from the Congolese point of view."

Van Rolse stood to his full height, his beard fluttering at his waist. "I think not," he said, the beard shaking. "You are provoking me."

The Count again raised his hands in a calming gesture. "Monsignor, God is not an old man sitting in the sky." Amazed yet again, Van Rolse stepped backwards. He was not accustomed to taking religious instruction from a government servant. He stood to his full height. "I suspect that God is an idea," continued the Count. "Without gender. Christ is an idea. Jesus embodied the Christ, but did not contain it."

"Our natives are black sons of Ham," the Monsignor declared. "God does not speak to them."

The Count continued to keep his hands upraised. "What if Christ, the idea, has bubbled up ever since Jesus was crucified? And authorities like you and me keep squelching it? And every time it tries to bubble up, that's a Second Coming?"

"And this Kimbangu is a manifestation of the Second Coming?" Van Rolse posed this question with astonishment. He started for the door. "This is heresy! Utter blasphemy!"

Count Lippens moved to block his way. "Must Christ come back looking like us? Otherwise it's heresy, blasphemy?"

The Monsignor looked with a kind of horror from the Count to the fetish. "Have you been consulting the fetish?" He turned to face it. "Get thee behind me, Satan!"

"Perhaps I should speak to Kimbangu," suggested the Count. "See if he is criminally insane."

"No!" shouted the churchman. "That's the last thing you want to do. It will credential him. He is a peasant, a native, a nothing. Suddenly the Governor-General asks to see him. Think of the status that gives him among savages. Don't see him! Squash him like a bug!"

This advice made the Governor-General shake his head.

"Act immediately," the Monsignor urged. "There's not a moment to lose."

The Count moved away from what seemed a madman. "I have not come to the Congo to squash Congolese. I will see for myself." He opened the door for the astonished Monsignor and closed it as soon as he passed through.

He went to his desk and sat on it. He put his hands to the sides of his head. Finally he sat down in his chair. He stared at the desktop. He had promised himself that he would not squash bugs. Still, the situation was rushing at him. He understood that he must act. As much as he hated to admit it, he knew that the raving churchman was right. He must stay out ahead of this prophet business. He called for Van Belle.

When the aide entered his office, he looked at him and shook his head. "You give me sober advice in a very sober way and I rejected it. This excited churchman offers counsel I'm inclined to take." He explained to Van Belle the action the Monsignor had recommended. Van Belle agreed with it. The Count instructed, "Send out an order to have Kimbangu taken into custody. Have him brought here." Contrary to the squash-the-bug advice, he added, "This is important. The prophet's not to be harmed. He's to be treated with dignity."

Van Belle said, "Right away, sir."

An hour later the Count left his office. Passing through that of his assistant, he asked Van Belle, "Was I too abrupt with the Monsignor?"

Van Belle smiled, but did not answer.

"I'm not kissing anyone's ring," declared the Count.

Van Belle nodded in agreement. "The Fathers get panicky at the slightest Congolese challenge to their Church," he explained. "Van Rolse is already upset because Protestants have translated the entire Bible for Congolese. How can the Fathers dominate the Congolese if they can read the Bible for themselves?"

"The Monsignor wants to play Governor-General."

"The Catholic Church is one of the interest groups that brings pressure to bear on us. It's a matter of balancing groups."

The Count tapped his fingers on the edge of the aide's desk. "Kimbangu and his people: are they one of these groups?"

"We don't ordinarily regard Congolese that way. It could happen."

"And how do I balance them?"

Van Belle grinned. "Very carefully. That might be even trickier than the Catholic Church."

"Good night, Van Belle." Mulling the order he had just given, the Count left the office and started down to the ground floor. Before he reached it, he turned around and hurried back upstairs. He re-entered Van Belle's office. "Let me change my instruction. This is a religious matter. Not a political one. It's premature to arrest Ki-- What?"

"Ki-mba-ngu, sir."

"Ki-mba-ngu. Yes, Kimbangu. Have-- Morel, is it?" Van Belle nodded. "Have him visit his village. See what's going on. Come give us a report." The Count left his aide's office and hurried downstairs.

It was good to be out in the air, to see the clouds reddened by sunset losing their color. He breathed deeply of the fresh air and strode to his residence. He climbed the stairs, thinking they might be very slippery when it rained.

At dinner the Countess said, "My dear, you must not provoke the Monsignor."

"What are you talking about?"

"And you should not dismiss him as you did."

The Count laughed, annoyed, surprised at what she knew. "I did not dismiss him," he said. "We had a gentleman's disagreement. How do you know about that?"

"Darling, nothing is secret in the Congo."

"That genuflecting fart. Clerical turd." His wife laughed. "Hasn't had an original idea in twenty years."

"That would be the original sin." They laughed together. The Countess added, "Van Rolse has been rather helpful with my research project." The Count looked confused. "About Kimpa Vita?"

"Oh, yes," muttered the Count. "Still, I will not have the Church telling me what to do."

The Countess changed her tone to issue a warning. "Be careful, my dear," she advised. "This situation is very delicate. Don't let some ignorant savage be your downfall." The Count liked hearing this advice from his wife only slightly better than from the cleric. But he knew that she was protecting his best interests. "Remember," she cautioned him. "The King is watching you. The prime minister's cabinet is watching you. They care nothing for a Congolese prophet. They are far away in Belgium, but they are watching."

Once again the Count raised his hands, this time in a gesture of supplication. Quietly he said, "They purposely appointed a man without previous colonial experience. They don't want things handled the way they've always been handled. 'Squash him like a bug.' This from a man of God!"

"Just remember," the Countess said, desiring the last word. "You want to come out of here in a way that enhances your interests. My interests. The family's interests. If that means being tough, don't falter. Do what must be done. The natives are not our brothers."

"Enough, my dear," he said. "I would like to dine in peace."

When the Countess concluded her research project, she reported, "Kimpa Vita was quite a girl. Simon Kimbangu cannot possibly be so colorful." She had visited the colonial archives and found nothing. However, when she consulted the Monsignor, he found for her a monograph written some years earlier by a historian-priest.

"Throughout her entire lifetime the Kingdom of the Kongo was wracked by civil war. She had youthful visions and had two early marriages that failed. She was not a docile wife."

The idea of a colorful, much-married vision-prone prophet amused the Count. Teasing his wife, he said, "The marriages must have set her on the path to ruin."

The Countess continued, "After the marriages – one of them produced a child - she took training that enabled her to communicate with the supernatural world." She looked up from her notes and saw her husband smiling. "By contrast, Kimbangu's entire background is Christian, *n'est-ce pas?*"

The couple were in their sitting room, enjoying coffee after dinner. The Countess examined her notes. "Let's see. She moved back toward Catholic precepts around 1700 when she was sixteen. She went to the abandoned capital of Sao Salvador with a group of pilgrims who wanted to end the ceaseless civil war."

The Countess went on, "Now here's fascinating stuff. She claimed to have seen a vision of St. Anthony of Padua. In recounting the vision to a priest, she died."

"Died?"

"That's how she described it. More coffee?" She leaned forward to glance into her husband's cup. It did not need refilling. "While dead, Kimpa Vita claimed, St. Anthony took over her body."

"Hmmm. Erotic stuff," said the Count, rolling his eyes. "An African ghost story!"

The Countess flicked her eyebrows. "She began to preach – with considerable success, I take it – and attracted followers. While this was happening – get this! – she claimed she died each Friday, spent the weekend in Heaven chatting with God" – wicked laughter began to interrupt the smooth flow of the Countess' narrative – "and then returned to earth on Mondays, just like a good shop girl." The Count joined her laughter. "Do you think it was a liaison?"

"Undoubtedly."

"She certainly meant her followers to think so."

"Why not? God must be even more virile than our nail fetish."

"I can hardly imagine that," said the Countess.

They chuckled together.

The Countess raised her hands to signal that she was not yet finished. She took a swallow of coffee to fortify herself and went on. "She designated St. Anthony as a second God and taught that Jesus, Mary and Anthony were all black-skinned Africans born in Kongo." The Countess raised her eyebrows. "Apparently after chatting with God, she preached that the civil wars angered Christ. They should stop and the Kingdom of Kongo become united under one ruler."

"She got political," observed the Count.

"She ran afoul of warring groups, got labeled a heretic, was captured, and burned at the stake."

"That must have seemed the easiest way to deal with her," observed the Count. "But did they have to kill her?"

"And her infant child?"

The Count laced his fingers together and placed them against his chin. After a moment he asked, "Did their killing her only complicate their problems?"

"Her influence lasted for some time," said the Countess.

The Count had grown meditative. "Did St. Joan have to be burned? And Paul and Peter executed? And Jesus?"

"You asked for this research to learn how these matters are handled in this area," said the Countess. She watched her husband for a long moment, then asked, "Do you see yourself already being maneuvered to execute Kimbangu?"

"I can see those forces already taking shape," he said. "But that's not going to happen. I will not let it. I've ordered one of our people to visit Kimbangu's village."

As Van Belle suggested, the Count's commutation of the Force Publique soldier's death sentence provoked criticism. Boma settlers complained that he was weak, lenient to Congolese. They stopped him on the streets of Boma to press him about the menace of Africans. Force Publique officers objected that unless discipline was rigidly enforced, other outrages, like Mbilo's attack on a white territorial administrator, would become commonplace. They assumed that soldiers all over the colony secretly wished to attack their masters. Monsignor Van Rolse stopped by the Governor-General's office to emphasize that commuting sentences was no way to stay ahead of the challenge Kimbangu presented.

Count Lippens maintained that the Free State era had seen too much killing; that was now a thing of the past. But the criticism continued. Opposition deepened. The Count decided to hunker down until Morel visited Nkamba and gave him a report about Kimbangu.

EIGHT

ÉON-GEORGES MOREL, NOT YET THIRTY, moved upward through the green hallway of Bas-Congo bush with steady, determined strides. He hoped that he exuded more confidence than he felt. Behind him along a sandy track walked a team of porters, carrying his tent and gear. The path was crowded with Africans, some singing, some jumping in a kind of ecstasy. Others limped along, hobbling on a single crutch. Still others carried the sick on palettes. Morel saw that some of those on palettes were sick unto death. Or, he thought, perhaps already dead. Did they expect Kimbangu to restore them to life?

The pilgrims moved forward as a swarm, their mood joyful with song and laughter. With expectation. Kimbangu had cracked open time itself. He had destroyed the past. A new era beckoned. Some pilgrims were marching toward a new world where the prophet would provide health and bounty for all. Others were moving toward a restoration of an idyllic yesteryear before the white man came.

As Morel strode along, news of his approach preceded him. As his entourage approached, the exultation quieted to a hush. Both the sick and the healthy hastened to the side of the path. In silence they watched the white man in his white uniform and white sun helmet with the curious prongs of hair that sprang from his upper lip in a handlebar mustache. Morel allowed his eyes to glance at the pilgrims, but he did not move his head. He marched, maintaining a posture that did not waver, his face, the visage of civilization, like indomitable force, pointed toward Nkamba.

Kimbangu's native village stood on a hilltop in hilly country. Morel found it so choked with people that his path into it grew ever narrower. Fewer revelers paid attention to him. As revelers they were gripped by a kind of rapture. They shuffled. They trembled. Their bodies shook. They sang at the top of their voices.

Morel's uniform announced him as a territorial officer. He expected to be greeted with the ceremony that befitted such a person. But the revelers ignored him. The commotion unnerved him. He gritted his teeth and strove to project confident authority. Entering the village he asked for directions to Kimbangu's dwelling and was led there. He ordered his porters to erect his tent within twenty yards of the dwelling.

He looked about expecting a village delegation to welcome him. Instead five people approached him: three men and two young girls. They sang, shouted bizarrely, so Morel thought, trembled, and whirled. They seemed without self-control. Morel stood erect and as tall as he could manage, hoping his white uniform, helmet and, most importantly, his white skin would protect him from any danger. He allowed the group to approach. The senior man presented himself.

Morel proclaimed, "I am seeking Simon Kimbangu."

The man standing before Morel, whom he had witnessed shouting, trembling, whirling, said, almost at full voice, "I am Kimbangu."

Morel was startled, but not impressed. The prophet seemed a man like any other. A bit taller than average, possessed of a certain presence. How could it be otherwise with crowds considering him a savior? Morel judged him to be suffering from some malady. What other conclusion could he draw when he himself was shown no respect?

An immense crowd gathered around them. Morel declared, "This is a grotesque and unsuitable way for you to receive a territorial administrator. Why are you and your people behaving like this?"

Speaking loudly, Kimbangu replied, "God ordered me to meet you this way."

"With shouting? Why all the shouting?"

Kimbangu informed him, "The shouts are the way I converse with God." Morel could hardly hear above the din. Kimbangu said, "God orders me and my followers to shout and tremble in this way."

Morel spent two nights at Nkamba, observing Kimbangu and the behavior of his followers. Kimbangu was not threatened; he was not harmed.

After his visit to Nkamba, Morel marched on to Gombe-Matadi. He lodged with missionaries there and was relieved to return to the company of people he understood. The missionaries told him that the expressions of Kimbangu and his followers replicated exactly the behavior of native witchdoctors of the past. So in that sense Kimbangu represented a return to a past that both territorial administrators and missionaries were trying to expunge.

When Morel returned to Cataracts-Sud, he prepared his report and received a summons to meet face-to-face with the Governor-General.

NINE

I F MOREL FELT INTIMIDATED BY THE ODD BEHAVIOR at Nkamba, he found the presence of the Governor-General equally unnerving. He wore a white uniform, newly washed and starched; he had cleaned his helmet and shoes; he had brushed his handlebar mustache. He tried to mask the nervousness he felt. That effort before people he respected, people who possessed control over him, was much more difficult than among people he regarded as savage. He found himself describing his visit to Nkamba, not only to the Governor-General in his office, but to Countess Joanna, Monsignor Van Rolse, the well-known planter Hans Bogaerts and the Governor's aide Van Belle.

Due to the criticism he was receiving among settlers, the Count had included the churchman and the planter. This was at Van Belle's suggestion. It was intended to preclude credible accusations that the administration had received information about Kimbangu that it was hiding. The two guests would learn the same information the Count received at the very time he received it. When they spread it to their contacts, they would have no reason to whisper that the Governor-General had intentions he was not disclosing.

Noticing his nervousness the Count invited Morel to give his report.

Morel began by describing his preparations, his porters and the route he took. He painted a word-picture of the festival atmosphere he encountered, the growing clamor the closer he moved to Nkamba. He noted that both the healthy and the ailing were making their way there. He mentioned the shuffling, the trembling, the singing, the shouting. He portrayed Kimbangu as a man of no special quality, apparently without self-control, an individual who might be mentally unbalanced. It was quite beyond his ability, he admitted, to understand how such a man could spellbind an entire community and set pilgrims on the march.

Listening to the report, Count Lippens wondered what background young Morel possessed that possibly warranted such opinions. It struck him that Morel was obviously a product of the colonial culture in which he lived and spent his days. He perceived that it was the same culture in which his guests spent their days. He remarked the enthusiasm with which those guests greeted the young man's assessments, judgments they themselves would have made about Kimbangu without ever meeting him. Van Rolse, for instance, continually referred to the prophet as a savage. The Count mulled the idea that he would be wise to make his own assessment of Kimbangu.

As Morel concluded his account of arriving at Nkamba, the Countess asked him to demonstrate the trembling he witnessed. The Count smiled privately, suspecting that his wife was bored; she was seeking entertainment, not edification.

Morel obliged her. Standing before the group, he whirled, writhed, and contorted his body in odd stances. His listeners beheld him, amazed. The Count glanced at his wife and saw devilment in her eyes.

To forestall her mischief he asked, "Is this trembling natural? Intentional or involuntary? Did these people seem possessed by spirits?"

"By the devil, don't you mean?" offered the Monsignor.

Morel said, "I saw followers who were trembling, foaming at the mouth, speaking in tongues. It was as if an epidemic of insanity had taken possession of the entire village."

"The devil dancing with them," remarked Van Rolse.

"With respect, sir," said Morel. "Kimbangu prohibits dancing. Shuffling, yes; dancing, no." This information startled his listeners. He continued, "He prohibits polygamy. And the use of fetishes."

"Isn't that what we're promoting?" asked the Count.

"Exactly," said Morel. "It's just like the missionaries."

The Monsignor grumbled, "The Fathers urge this and are ignored. Kimbangu urges it and they obey." He turned to Morel. "Is that what you're telling us? Is it true? You observed that?"

"Yes, Monsignor. I saw no fetishes." Morel continued, "People were shouting hymns. Kimbangu says that hymns must be sung loudly, enthusiastically, because then he is given the power of healing. The louder the song, the stronger the spirit comes."

"Was there healing?" asked Van Belle.

"Nkamba is full of sick people," Morel stated. "And many are healed. People are leaving hospitals to have Kimbangu heal them. I saw people bringing corpses to the village."

A cry of disgust escaped the Countess's throat.

"The natives know very well," Morel went on, "that we will never approve of the grotesque and insane displays that accompany their worship."

"But isn't that proper?" asked the Count. "If Kimbangu acted like us, like a European, his people would not believe in him. Isn't this true?" The Count thought this a most reasonable assumption. He looked to Van Belle for agreement. The aide only shrugged.

"What do you think he's up to?" the planter asked Morel.

As if he were an authority the young officer stated, "He intends to create a religion for the African mentality. Animism with a dollop of the Protestantism he knows. Toss in some fetishism, though I saw none." Morel became almost professorial. "European religions are filled with abstractions. That doesn't work for the African. He longs for concrete facts and protection."

The Count saw how quickly one of his administrators could become an expert. He noted how readily a junior officer was believed when his remarks mirrored the beliefs his listeners already held.

Morel moved to the Count's nail fetish. "This fellow is not an abstraction," he continued. "To the African mind he embodies power. Kimbangu may eschew fetishes. Still, his teachings provide palpable facts: healings, protection against sickness. His movement is pan-African. The natives want a God of the blacks and think that he is it. To them he is the Second Coming."

The Monsignor looked aghast.

Planter Bogearts turned to face the Count. "Move against it!" he demanded.

Morel continued, "Other prophets are popping up, the *n'gunza*. Kimbangu has rejected many of them as false. But he has also appointed twelve apostles."

The Monsignor cried, "What blasphemy!"

"These prophets have begun to baptize," declared Bogaerts. "They urge people to withhold their taxes. They spread chaos throughout the countryside. My workers have left the plantations. How can we build a new society if all the natives run off?"

"But wouldn't you do the same," asked the Countess, "if you thought he was the Second Coming?" The Count rewarded her with a smile.

"They all need to be exiled, the whole lot!" contended Bogaerts.

"This is not simply the problem of Kimbangu," said the Monsignor. "But of all these prophets. These *n'gunza*. If they accept Kimbangu as the Second Coming, they must be stopped."

"This is leading to rebellion," declared Bogaerts.

The Count turned to Morel. "Do they speak against the state?"

"Not Kimbangu, sir. But these others, self-seekers, some of them certainly do. They talk of Garveyism, a contagion from America."

"Pan-Negro-ism," explained the churchman. "Very dangerous."

For the first time Van Belle spoke. "Kimbangu may be a man of the Spirit," he said. "The *n'gunza* are something else."

"Exile them!" proposed Bogaerts. "Send them to the farthest reaches of the territory."

"Or find other means of getting rid of them," offered the Monsignor.

The Count felt the meeting slipping out of his control. He was alarmed at how quickly it went from a description of Nkamba to cries for "getting rid" of individuals.

Morel said, "As a person, Kimbangu struck me as being very ill. I would urge him to go to hospital for observation."

"Don't 'urge' him," cried Bogaerts, fixing the eyes of one person, then moving to the next. "Hospitalize him! Get him out of circulation." After peering at each of the others, he stopped at the Governor-General. "Before we have a revolt on our hands," he urged. "Who knows what they are planning?"

"Count, you must do something," agreed the Monsignor.

"If they only understood how few we are!" moaned Bogaerts. "What are the whites in the Congo? Thirty-five hundred? They could so easily overwhelm us!"

That, thought the Count, was the real problem: too few colonials trying to hold onto too vast a prize. Masked behind protestations of a civilizing mission, that had been the strategy of Leopold II. When he had accepted the post, the Count had not realized how nakedly that was the task: to hold onto the prize.

"What do you propose I do?" he asked. Maybe that question would allow him to regain control of the meeting.

"Exile the lot of them," urged the Monsignor. "Certainly the n'gunza. And arrest Kimbangu. Charge him!"

"With what?" asked the Count. "Healing the sick? Raising the dead?"

The churchman once again urged that the Count charge Kimbangu with sedition. Bogaerts suggested with sowing rebellion. The churchman proposed a trial. Naturally Kimbangu would be found guilty. The planter preferred execution. The Count shook his head. He explained, "Such an act would provoke the very rebellion we hope to prevent."

The planter said, "Governor-General, you are too lenient with these fellows."

"Squash the bug!" shouted the Monsignor.

When the Count realized that excitement about execution had taken over the meeting, he declared it at an end. He asked Van Belle to see his guests out. The two visitors shook hands with everyone, informing the Count sotto voce that he must take action.

The Countess withdrew to allow her husband time to speak with Morel in private. Once they were alone, the Count wanted a break from talking about Kimbangu. He had come to suspect that the morale of the territorial administrators was crucial to colonial progress. He asked Morel about his situation. What were his lodgings? Were they satisfactory? How were his servants? Did he have a decent cook? Was he eating well enough? Did he get adequate sleep? "All of this is important in terms of the job you do."

"I hope my service is up to the grade," said Morel.

The Count inquired, "Do you find it lonely?" Morel shrugged. "Do you have ways of getting female companionship from time to time?"

The young officer seemed flummoxed as to how he should answer this question.

"Find a woman to take care of you," advised the Count. "That's not unimportant. Men without women sometimes come down too hard on the people they supervise. I trust you've heard of this man Sambry who made such a mess of things."

"I have, sir," said Morel.

"We don't want that happening, do we? So take care of that matter if you haven't already done so."

"I'll take that as an instruction, sir." Morel laughed, a bit embarrassedly. "I'll get to it."

"And as for Kimbangu," said the Count, "what are your recommendations?"

"If I may say so, sir," Morel began. "I believe inaction could lead to problems." He proposed that the government act before Kimbangu's movement – and, more importantly, the *n'gunza* movement which sprang from it – could spread. "That could create difficulties for the administration," he supposed. "I think it crucial that we remove Kimbangu from his base at Nkamba. Isolate him." House arrest would provoke outcries, he acknowledged. But hospitalization could be explained as an effort to stabilize Kimbangu's health after the stressful and turbulent time. It could be indefinite. The credibility of the explanation might be questioned, he assumed, but Leopold II could point the way. He had done what he wanted in the Free State era by proclaiming himself to be a humanitarian, fighting the slave trade.

"I doubt that's the way to go," replied the Count. "We're trying new approaches in the colony." He instructed Morel to remain overnight in Boma and consider what they had discussed. He would announce his intentions in the morning.

Alone in his office, the Count stared out the window at his thoughts. He sat at his desk, trying to decide the most reasonable and most effective policy. The most reasonable policy might be to place a *cordon sanitaire* around Nkamba, withhold access to the place, proscribe the transport of the sick to the village as a threat to public health and let the excitement wear itself out. Even the possessed got tired. But would that be effective? Would it satisfy the settlers with their appetite for vigorous action? To arrest a prophet for healing struck the Count as ludicrous. It was an abdication of his responsibilities to Congolese.

But in this environment healing was a political act. There was no denying that. The Count wondered if it were credible for the administration to offer Kimbangu protection. But from what? European paranoia? Providing that protection might require arresting him.

At dinner the Count asked his wife, "What did you think of Morel?"

"Out of his depth."

"You could say that of all of us. Certainly of me."

"It was perceptive of you to suggest he find a woman."

"You were listening at the door again. You really must not do that," he chastised.

"Do you think he can find one?" she asked. "I'm not sure he can. It's the wrong face for that ridiculous mustache. You should advise him to shave it off." She pantomimed shaving off a luxuriant growth of hair.

"No, no!" shouted the Count, laughing. "That mustache is essential to his identity." He vigorously flicked his eyebrows. "With that mustache preceding him," he said, "Morel has the courage to walk into Kimbangu's village and to be thought the most important man there. Impressive."

"And to do that shuffle. That took some courage."

The Count chuckled at the memory of Morel's bizarre exhibition. "You were naughty to invite him to perform for us."

"I wanted to see his mustache wiggle. Very erotic."

"It gave him the courage to tell that Richelieu Van Rolse that Kimbangu prohibited dancing and fetishes. Not easy to stick to your guns in the face of that unmovable object."

"And to suggest the fellow only be hospitalized for eternity and not squashed like a bug. I suppose he wasn't so bad."

After a moment the Count asked, "What do I do about Van Rolse and Bogaerts?"

"Execute them!" suggested his wife. "Exile them to the farthest borders of the realm!"

"Excellent proposals!" said the Count. "I thank you for them."

That evening as the Lippenses were preparing for bed, the Countess emerged from the bathroom wearing a lightweight nightgown held onto her shoulders by two narrow straps. The Count was in bed, reading a report. He glanced up and gave her a smile. She looked at him with wickedness in her eyes. Her expression excited her husband's distrust, but also intrigued him, since she had smeared mascara across her upper lip. The smear resembled a handlebar mustache.

The Countess began to tremble, satirizing the movements Morel had shown them earlier in the day. She trembled mightily. She shook. She whirled. She jumped about. Her nightgown began to slip off her body. She shook faster, with greater determination. The nightgown fell to the floor. She stepped out of it, naked, and kept trembling, shaking, whirling.

Delighted, her husband slipped out of bed and joined her, whirling, trembling, shaking. He untied the cord holding his pajamas to his waist. Shaking with more determination, he managed to tumble them to the floor.

Together the Count and Countess danced, shook, trembled. She moved with abandon, her breasts and buttocks swaying. Naked from the waist down, the Count's masculinity swung to and fro. It grew erect. He pulled the pajama top off his chest, held it above his head, and twirled it. They danced closer together. They clasped one another. Kissed. Broke the kiss. The Countess picked up her nightgown and tossed it across a chair. The Count reached out, took his wife's hand, and led her to their bed.

The next morning at the office the Count consulted Van Belle. "I did a lot of thinking last night," he told his assistant. "Bogaerts, the Monsignor, and others already half-hysterically expect a black tide to overwhelm us."

Van Belle smiled his agreement. "They see reasons for being afraid behind every bush," he said. "I suspect the Congolese excitement about Kimbangu is simply a different expression of religion. No more."

Count Lippens observed, "We can't arrest his followers for not being European. But I would not be surprised if the Monsignor is already writing warnings of Armageddon to the palace in Brussels."

"Indeed, he may be."

"He'll force my hand."

Van Belle added, "The *n'gunza* are a different matter."

The Count meditatively drummed his fingers on his desk. He thought he'd be damned if he'd allow the cleric to usurp his power, to force him into actions he felt overblown. Still he realized he must do something – but with restraint. At the same time his cautious side reminded him that discretion was wiser than moving into a confrontation with the church. So it might be well to let Van Rolse win the first skirmish. He hoped it did not become a battle, but it might. "I'm afraid we must be seen to act," he said. "We must do something."

Count Lippens stared out the window at the green tangle of the countryside. He asked Van Belle to fetch Morel.

When the young officer presented himself, the Count at first noticed only the handlebar mustache. Looking more carefully he saw that the young man appeared robust and revitalized, less nervous in his manner. Perhaps his advice had done some good. He wondered if Morel had patronized a brothel.

The Count declared, "I think it's wise for us to remove Kimbangu from his village." Morel agreed. "But carefully," stressed the Count. "If we invite him to meet us in Thysville and he ignores us, that's defiance. It demands that we retaliate." The Count studied Morel and wondered if he were capable of the task he had in mind for him. "We don't want to excite his followers. That will only trigger opposition."

Morel said, "Yes, sir."

The Count went on, "I see no alternative to arresting him." His eyes bore in on the young officer. "That's your task, Morel." The young man rose to his full height, signaling that he was ready for any assignment. "Take a detachment of Force Publique," instructed the Count. "Plan carefully how you intend to move. Kimbangu will be surrounded by followers. They will oppose you. Let no one be hurt. We don't want this blowing up in our faces." He asked, "Anything to add, Van Belle?"

Van Belle turned to face Morel. "It's important that no one is hurt," he said. "Especially not Kimbangu."

"Thank you both," said the Count, concluding the meeting. "Have a good journey back to your post, Morel. Move against Nkamba in a way that guarantees success."

Morel saluted him.

After he and Van Belle departed, the Count paced back and forth across the office, doubtful that the young man was up to the task. He wondered if he had sent him on a fool's errand. Trying to arrest Kimbangu in that village crowded with excited followers... Those followers would do all they could to protect their prophet… He had given Morel an almost impossible task, one he felt under pressure to order. He asked himself: Was it really necessary to let Van Rolse win the first skirmish?

TEN

ÉON-GEORGES MOREL MARCHED THROUGH jungle vegetation leading a detachment of Force Publique soldiers. The only white man in what might be a thousand square miles, he felt very alone. He knew his mission was futile. Did the Governor-General actually expect it to succeed? He liked the man well enough, but he'd been in the colony so short a time. Had he ever been outside of Boma? Had he ever entered a village?

Marching on, Morel thought about women. "Find a woman to take care of you!" advised the Governor-General. How he would love to do that! He would love to sleep regularly with a woman. What a relief that would be!

But he must think about this mission, Morel reminded himself. How, he wondered, could he possibly arrest Simon Kimbangu? The knowledge that he would fail depressed him. The soldiers under his command must be sensing his nervousness, his depression.

Morel wondered: What would the Governor-General regard as an "adequate detachment"? Did he assume his men were actually trained? In fact, they were still getting used to wearing boots. They hardly understood what it meant to carry a lethal weapon, shoot at a person, actually hit him, and cause his death. Morel feared that in the heat of confrontation, his men would fire their weapons despite receiving strict orders not to.

The men had been apprised of their mission: to surround the village of Nkamba, enter it without provoking confrontation, and pluck from it the leader of what was by now a mob of religious devotees. The mob would be fanatically loyal to that leader and prepared to defend him with their lives.

Morel wondered: Did his soldiers believe the mission could be accomplished? Given its futility, he asked himself, what exactly constituted his authority over the men? Shouted orders? The force of arms? But the soldiers had the arms. Merely the whiteness of his skin? Did the men realize that the mission was sure to fail? Probably.

Morel's mustache twitched on his upper lip. Moving well ahead of the soldiers, he grew aware of the hubbub of Nkamba, the ululations, the raucous hymn singing. He heard shuffling that had the rhythms and appearance of dancing although the devotees did not regard it as dance because dancing was forbidden. There was the constant shaking, the trembling; it seemed to cause a shivering of the very vegetation through which the detachment marched.

The soldiers encountered the lame, the halt and the dying; they were seemingly discarded at the sides of the path. The devotees heard the soldiers approaching. The jungle suddenly went silent.

At the edge of Nkamba Morel halted his men. Activity ceased. Women left off pounding manioc to flour in pestles. They shooed children into huts. They stopped spreading laundry over bushes to dry. They turned to watch. Men guarded pathways to protect their families. The village lay in soundless waiting.

Morel felt the watchfulness of the villagers like a weight on his shoulders. He tasted dryness in his mouth. He wondered how many village men had weapons. Using arm signals, he directed his soldiers to take up positions at every pathway into the village center.

Morel and two sergeants moved slowly into the village itself. Several paces behind them his soldiers advanced. The villagers observed them, motionless. Morel's sergeants asked for Simon Kimbangu. They inquired repeatedly for the prophet. No villager spoke. They watched in silence.

Morel led the men toward Kimbangu's dwelling. Everywhere silence. He approached the house. He extended his fist to knock at the door. His fist struck wood.

Pandemonium broke loose. Shrieks shredded the air. Voices ululated, raised hymns, shouted prayers. Villagers ran to and fro. They scurried this way and that. They buffeted soldiers, obstructed their movement.

A rifle fired.

A cold wave of panic swept through Morel. More shooting. Morel ordered it to stop. He shouted the order again and again. At last the firing ended.

The paroxysm of shouting and rushing about finally quieted. The village was silent again - except for the keening of a woman. She approached Morel. Her shoulder spouted blood. She carried a baby; its small body burbled blood. She showed the baby to Morel. It had been shot. It was dead.

Merde! Oh, merde! thought Morel. A wounded woman and a baby we've killed.

He ordered the medic to bandage the woman. He gathered his men. He tried to discover who had shot her. No soldier would acknowledge responsibility. It was foolish to badger the men with an inquiry. Perfunctorily they began to search for Kimbangu. Morel knew they would not find him. He realized that as night fell the villagers would gain the advantage. They might seek revenge. He withdrew the detachment. Marching in retreat he tried to devise the best way to tell his superiors what had happened.

ELEVEN

WHEN THE COUNT LEARNED THAT MOREL'S MISSION to Nkamba had failed, he was not surprised. He reported to his wife that Kimbangu had escaped and vanished. She wondered if this were a calamity or a Godsend. She knew her husband wished the Kimbangu problem did not exist. She sensed that he feared that pressure from both the Catholic Church and the settlers would force him to deal with the prophet in a manner he utterly rejected.

"Isn't it just as well that he's escaped arrest?" the Countess asked over dinner. "You can't have expected that mission to succeed."

"It was a bone thrown to the Monsignor," he admitted. His wife shuddered. A grin appeared on his lips. "You won't mention that if you go to confession, will you?"

"I only confess to being short-tempered with the servants. And swearing now and then at the heat."

"Excellent. Keep it that way."

With Kimbangu's whereabouts unknown, the Count could continue to devote his energies to the enormous project of reordering the *chefferies,* the entities of native rule, throughout the colony. The next time he met General LeMoine of the Force Publique he suggested that hunting Kimbangu need not have high priority. It was more important that the Force work to see that the reassignment of chiefs not be allowed to get out of hand.

"When you see him next, I hope you won't be too hard on Officer Mustache," said the Countess.

"I must feign some disappointment," the Count replied. "I must be careful. My reactions are reported throughout the town."

"Who reports them?" asked the Countess.

"Maybe air currents."

"Van Belle?"

"I hope not."

The Count ordered that Morel should come to Boma to give a report and promptly pushed the mission's failure to the back of his mind.

A week later when Van Belle showed Morel into the Governor-General's office, the young man stood stiffly to his full height. He felt very nervous. The Count examined him from boots to eyebrows and said, "What happened?"

"I take full responsibility, sir."

The Count could see that Morel had carefully considered how to present himself. He felt sympathy for the man, who reminded him a bit of his elder son. "Do relax," he urged.

"The good news," Morel began, "is that we have arrested a number of *n'gunza*, the lesser prophets. They've been exiled to penal camps. They were preaching against the state."

"What about Kimbangu, man?"

"Our detachment was too small," said Morel.

"You need a battalion to arrest one man?"

"We needed more men than we had," said Morel. "The Force Publique detachment was essential. But it made Kimbangu flee."

"I acknowledge it was a difficult mission," said the Count. No detachment of Force Publique, led by an inexperienced officer, was likely to whisk a prophet away from his village. Not when his followers regarded him as the Second Coming. But the Count thought it was unnecessary to mention that. He inquired, "Did Kimbangu escape before you arrived? Or once you were there?"

"I'm not sure what happened," Morel admitted. "The place just exploded. If Kimbangu was there, that's when he left."

An unsatisfactory report, thought the Count, even given the mission's difficulty. Morel should know what went wrong. He glanced at Van Belle; his expression was impassive. "Is there more?" he asked.

"The detachment did some shooting," Morel admitted. "A baby was killed. Its mother was injured. We bandaged her up."

The Count frowned to show his irritation.

Van Belle observed, "Kimbangu's escape enhances his reputation."

The Count nodded.

"We searched for him," Morel assured him. "He's vanished into the bush. He won't be easy to find."

"Efforts to find him," the Count said, "will only provoke unrest. We don't want that. Any idea of what he's up to now?"

"Our best intelligence is that he's moving around the region, spreading his teachings."

"And his teachings are what?" asked the Count.

"Lead moral lives. No polygamy. No dancing."

"Politics?"

"Not so far as I know," said Morel. "The *n'gunza* do politics and we arrest them."

"Good," replied the Count. Then with prudence he asked, "If Kimbangu refrains from preaching against the state, doesn't it serve our purposes to let him stay in hiding?"

This idea surprised both Van Belle and Morel. The Count rose from his desk and began to pace the room. He cautiously proposed, "If he's preaching a kind of African Christianity not much different from what the missionaries preach, doesn't it make sense for us to let him be?"

The two listeners regarded him with perplexity. "Are you suggesting that as policy?" asked Van Belle?

"I'm thinking out loud," said the Count.

Morel blurted, "The settlers want protection—"

"But from what?" asked the Count, still pacing. "He isn't harming them."

"They're nervous that—"

"But they think he's harming them. Or will be," said Van Belle.

"I'm not willing to have the Force Publique go chasing this fellow simply because some settlers are nervous." The Count stopped pacing and faced his listeners. They both looked at the floor.

Finally Morel found enough courage to say, "My recommendation is that the Force Publique should occupy Nkamba."

Van Belle gave a laugh, relaxing a bit, and said, "I'm afraid our compatriots will scream if we don't at least do that."

"Do we really want troops occupying a village?" The Count posed the question as if it made him incredulous. "The way we're handling this, we're our own worst enemies. If we appease the settlers and the Catholic Church, this business is going to bite us."

The men were silent, awaiting direction from the Count. He saw that they anticipated his instructions. He had none to give.

"Thank you, gentlemen," he finally said. "We'll have to handle this the best way we can. Let's just be sure we think before we act." As the men were leaving the office, the Count said, "Morel, could you stay a moment?"

Morel stopped, tried to mask the shudder that slithered down his spine, and turned back toward the Count, trying to smile.

The Count observed him almost paternally. "Would you care to have lunch with the Countess and me?" he asked.

An expression of relief jumped onto the young man's face so quickly that he had no opportunity to mask it. He smiled, laughed with the joy of escape. "That would be a great honor, sir. Thank you."

"Good. Why don't you appear at the residence at, say, one o'clock. Don't worry. It will be very casual."

"At one o'clock, sir. Thank you."

After Morel withdrew, the Count walked about his office. Eventually he stood before the nail fetish. He stared at it for a long moment. Then he turned his back on the sculpture and sat at his desk, pondering the problem of Kimbangu, certain it was actually a problem of settlers, the church, and probably plantation owners as well.

As Morel passed through Van Belle's office, he hesitated. Van Belle raised his eyes from what he was doing. Timidly Morel said, "The Governor-General invited me to lunch. What does that mean?"

Van Belle smiled. "I have no idea. He has never invited me to lunch."

"Really?" Morel looked surprised.

Van Belle shook his head.

"Does he mean to ride me out in private?"

"That's possible," the assistant agreed. "He has a certain—" He hesitated, undecided about how to express himself. He shrugged, plunged ahead. "He's of the nobility, you know. Has a certain upper class way of handling things." Van Belle watched the young man grow terrified before his eyes. "'Nobility' means whatever he does, it's not meant to frighten you," he said reassuringly. "Some G-Gs would want to frighten you. But not this one, I think."

"Thank you." Morel moved through the door.

Van Belle called to his retreating figure, "Have a good lunch."

The Count had a purpose in extending an invitation to Morel. He had been thinking more and more about making young men into effective officers. As he considered the reforms he needed to achieve, he realized the importance of shaping the men who would oversee them. To re-order the Free State *chefferie* system, some chiefs would become surplus. Which meant that they must be dealt with by administrators in such a way that they did not resist the colonial administration.

Territorial administrators, originally hired by the Free State, usually lacked the time and the skills – patience and tact – to effect this transition. It was one thing to know what needed to be achieved; it was quite another to encourage and inspire young men like Morel to actually achieve it. Given the case of Sambry, the Count had realized that shaping the men who administered the colony demanded attention. They needed to be efficient, of course, but they must also understand that they were serving Africans as well as controlling them. Serving Africans was an idea that would take months to inculcate. As a result, dealing with Kimbangu was a problem well down the list.

Lunching with Morel was a way to explore attacking the challenge of shaping a stronger corps of territorial administrators.

At the residence the Count asked his wife, "You remember young Morel of the mustache?" The Countess gave an imitation of a tremble. "You remember I sent him off to arrest the prophet?"

"He made a mess of it."

"More or less. I invited him to lunch. At one o'clock. Can Cook set a place for him?"

"Of course. Are we talking Kimbangu?"

"I think the topic is: How to survive the bush."

When Morel arrived at the residence and met Countess Joanna, he apologized for appearing without flowers or chocolates, gifts he had been trained to offer an important hostess. "I don't know where to get such things in Boma."

"I don't know that they exist here," said the Countess. "We're still very new in Africa."

Morel's apology pleased the Count. It suggested that Morel had a background from which an effective officer could be molded. The Count would explore such molding at lunch.

There he led the trio to talk about Morel's life in the bush, his daily activities, his interaction with Africans, his being called upon occasionally to settle disputes. "I'm realizing more and more," acknowledged the Count, "that if we have the right men in the field, things go well. If we have the wrong men, things go badly. So we must remake them if we can into the right sort of men."

"Tell us about your domestic life," suggested the Countess as they ate their desserts. "Do you actually have one? Is there a social life?"

"I don't really have a domestic life," acknowledged Morel. "I live in the back of my office. Sometimes I play cards with a missionary nearby."

"Did you leave a girl – perhaps a fiancée – at home?" asked the Count.

Morel openly drew into himself.

"Is that a delicate subject?" asked the Countess.

Morel shrugged. "There was a girl. We talked about marriage. But when I went into the colonial service, she refused me."

"I'm so sorry," said the Countess.

"I suppose I should have expected it," Morel admitted. "For the first months out here I missed her very much." He looked at his hands, annoyed with himself for confessing so much, for letting emotion sound in his voice.

While they finished their dessert, they moved to other subjects. As the Countess poured them coffee – they had adjourned to the small parlor – the Count recalled, "I believe I suggested to you at one point that you find a young woman to take care of you."

"Yes, sir, you did." The young man looked embarrassed.

"And have you found one?"

"I'm going to excuse myself for a few moments," declared the Countess. "I need to thank Cook for our lunch."

As she rose from her chair, Morel rose, too, very conscious of his manners. Once she was gone, he sat down again. While he was on his feet the Count watched him, both benevolently and amused.

"Don't be embarrassed," said the Count. "Our women are very aware that the right companion settles a man. It helps him become a better officer."

"I wish I knew how to go about it," Morel confessed. Neither man spoke for a moment for the Count himself did not really know how a young man might go about finding a native woman he'd actually want to live with.

Finally the Count offered, "Celibacy is not an answer."

"No," Morel agreed quietly.

"Neither is trying to take care of things yourself."

This observation embarrassed Morel. He stared at his hands.

"Rebellion against attempted celibacy is often violent."

Morel smiled. "But unfortunately there are no matchmakers in this place."

"At least not for colonial officers." After a moment the Count asked, "Would you want a settler's daughter?"

"Gad, no!" Morel laughed. "A settler's daughter would see where I live and complain round the clock. I might kill her."

"So how do we find you an African-- Maiden?" The Count smiled as he said the word. Morel smiled, too. He had not thought that an African girl for his bed would be a "maiden." "Once you find her, you'd have to treat her decently, you know." Morel nodded. "I'm told many native men beat their women."

"From what I've seen, they do."

"How did your father treat your mother?" the Count asked. Morel looked surprised, even offended, by this question. "That's probably how you'd treat your woman."

"I wouldn't beat her. I don't hit women."

"If you didn't beat her, she would think herself very lucky. She'd realize she'd landed well." Then after a pause, "Did your father yell at your mother?"

"Not often. She yelled back."

"You wouldn't want a girl who put on airs, being Morel's woman."

Morel shook his head.

"Probably from the dominant tribe in your area. A girl from a lesser tribe might have difficulties."

Morel laughed. "Should I be taking notes?"

"What kind of girl would you want?"

Morel considered the question, then replied. "Pretty. I'd be looking at her a lot. Slim. Not skinny, but not—"

"What qualities besides how she looks?"

Morel thought for a moment. "Quiet, I guess. Maybe I mean self-possessed. Not flighty. A sense of humor, though I don't imagine we'd be telling each other jokes. Clean. A good housekeeper. A good cook although maybe the man who cooks for me would stay on." He shrugged. "Responsive in bed, of course." The Count nodded. "Though not given to too much of that."

Morel and the Count regarded one another, Morel trying to think of other necessary qualities. "She should speak some French," Morel added. "She could teach me Lingala."

The Count smiled. "Now all we have to do is find her." The Count folded his arms across his chest and gazed at the ceiling, trying to think where this maiden could be found. He thought, of course, of asking Van Belle. But, having once probed Van Belle's domestic arrangements, he carefully avoided mentioning them again. He had an African woman, most unmarried white men did, but the Count regarded this as none of his affair. Still, Van Belle served as his main source on how native society worked.

The Countess rejoined the men to find them silent and apparently deep in thought. "Am I interrupting something?" she asked, seating herself in the chair she had occupied before.

The Count explained what he and Morel had been discussing. "I'm afraid such a discussion in your presence embarrasses this young man," the Count said. "But we are thinking of his health." Morel blushed. "Where would we find him a companion?"

"Go where such girls are," said the Countess as if it were the most obvious answer.

"And where are they?" asked Morel.

"Are there convent schools near where you're stationed?" she asked.

This seemed a new idea to Morel.

"Go to the Mother Superior," advised the Countess. "Explain that you need a companion. That the Governor-General himself" – the Count looked surprised at this – "suggested that you try this school. Emphasize that satisfying your need for companionship will benefit not only yourselves – of course, you must make her see that it benefits the girl – but the region where you serve and the colony as a whole. A colonial official with a companion is better than one who is lonely and irritable and short-tempered as a result. I'm sure she will find you a girl who will please you."

"And with that good advice," said the Count, "I must get back to work."

He and Morel walked back together as far as the State House. As they parted, the Count instructed the young man, "Think about what my wife suggested. I think it's a very good idea."

At dinner the Countess remarked, "I never expected that we would play matchmaker for bachelor officials."

"I rather like Morel," said the Count, "despite the mustache. If a companion makes his service easier and more efficient, why not try to help that happen?"

"What about the other 'lost boys' in your colonial service?"

"Let them all find companions. Let them have regular sex in a structured environment. Let some of them fall in love with their consorts and realize that Africans are real people." He sat back expansively and made a prediction. "Sex will settle them down." He smiled, teasing her. "Look what it's done for me."

"But I'm a white woman, in case you hadn't noticed. Settlers' wives and probably your good friend the Monsignor will be horrified to think that you are championing savage, inter-racial sex."

"Let them be horrified. I'm sure sex with nubile black girls trained to please a man is much better than it is with some of these settlers' daughters trained to make a man's life miserable." The Countess laughed and nodded in agreement. "And as for the Monsignor I would recommend exactly the same thing for him – if he's not already enjoying it. As I feel certain many of his village priests are doing."

"I didn't know you thought so much about sex," observed the Countess, raising an eyebrow in an extraordinarily provocative way.

"I do think about it – for the 'lost boys' as well as the 'lost men.'" It was clear he considered himself among this latter group. "And if you are not careful that dangerous eyebrow will entice me to pick you up and take you to our bedroom."

The Countess laughed and continued to flick her eyebrow.

TWELVE

IN THE *CHEFFERIE* REFORM THAT COUNT LIPPENS was directing the neighboring *chefferies* of Nsona and Nkandu had been combined into a single
entity now called Nkonzo. Hitherto Nsona had been led by a hereditary
chief named Bézo while Nkandu's chief was a young man Koté who had risen
in the ranks of the Force Publique to the position of sergeant. Since he had
picked up some Flemish while in the Force and had some understanding of
Belgians and how their territorial administration worked, Koté was chosen
to head up the combined *chefferie* Nkonzo. As a result of the amalgama-
tion, Nsona's hereditary chief Bézo was disgruntled, angry that a young man
without the correct lineage or experience of tribal administration should be
permitted to oust him from the chieftaincy he deserved. As a result, Koté saw
that he must take some action to strengthen his position with the people of
the new *chefferie* Nkonzo.

As it happened, a situation arose which perfectly fit Koté's requirements.
A new territorial administrator, young in the colonial service, had arrived in
the area. Once he had settled in and the isolation of his circumstances began
to press down on him, a social person, he found his loneliness excruciating.
To escape it he ordered Force Publique soldiers to send him their wives. These
women cooked his dinner and spent the night, serving as sexual outlets.

His lying with their wives angered the soldiers. At first they tolerated this
practice because they had been trained to follow the white man's orders. But
when Koté learned of these practices, he quickly recognized the opportunity
they presented.

He complained about them to his contacts in the Force Publique. Skeptical of the complaints, for such behavior was an outrage, officers of the Force
nonetheless reported them to the territorial administration. Administrators
investigated and discovered not only that the complaints were true, but also
that on an earlier occasion the young administrator, Sambry by name, had
been involved with a Congolese woman, a soldier's wife. He had suffered an
attack, now called "near fatal," from a soldier.

Sambry was a bad egg. The area's chief administrator placed him under
house arrest and had him guarded. He was soon to stand trial.

When vice-Governor-General Baron Thibaud communicated this news
to Count Lippens, the Count was furious. He could reluctantly excuse the

first incident on the basis that Sambry was new to the colony and that reports of the incident's circumstances were confused. But Sambry should have learned a lesson and the soldier Mbilo was in prison. The Count considered the present charges intolerable. He told his wife, "Your friend Sambry has committed more intolerable acts."

"What makes you think he's a friend of mine?" asked the Countess. "Is it a black man's woman again?"

"Several. He seems to have been working his way through all the women of a Force Publique detachment."

"It gets lonesome in the bush," she observed, teasing.

"He should taste the bite of a rhino hide whip."

In suggesting this punishment the Count was serious, but when he discussed the matter with Van Belle, his aide insisted that settlers would be appalled at the use of a chicotte on a white man. "African skin is tougher," he contended. "Two lashes on a white man's back would scar him for life." Again Van Belle advised the Count to escape criticism by not intervening.

The Count replied to Baron Thibaud that Sambry must be punished in a manner that would be clear as punishment to the aggrieved soldiers. He wrote, "Sambry is not to be sent back to Belgium until he has faced punishment in the colony. Keep me informed."

If Sambry's behavior infuriated the Count, it also set him to thinking. What did he really know of the Congo? Of its two hundred tribes speaking two hundred languages? Had he any real inkling of how they lived? How they thought? His administration was sending lusty, inexperienced young men who did not have strong Christian values, strong Belgian values – whatever that meant – to reorder the way Africans lived. He felt relieved that there were not more problems in the bush than those he was aware of. But what percentage did he know about? What percentage, even more egregious, were being hidden from him? He allowed these thoughts to join him and the Countess at the dinner table.

He asked her, "Do you sometimes feel that we are rather silly sitting here on this estuary assuming that we are actually governing?"

The Countess teased him. "I have never supposed I was doing any governing. Men do that, don't they? We merely watch them do it, feeling rather proud of themselves."

"Is that what you really think of me?" the Count asked, somewhat offended.

"Didn't I say, 'Present company excepted, of course?'" she replied, smiling.

"I suppose we are doing our *petit possible.*"

The Count persisted, only slightly annoyed at the teasing. "This Sambry business..." he said. "This advice we've given Morel... They've made me realize that I have no idea what the rigors of the bush are like. I wonder if I will ever understand anything about the Congo if I allow myself to be cooped up in Boma. We admire ourselves for tolerating the privations of this African capital. And who could suggest that it is not much more rustic than homes we've had in Flanders? But I can't fool myself about this. I haven't even penetrated fifty kilometers into the vastness of this colony I'm governing." He concluded, "I must see some of the country. Would you come with me on a little jaunt? Or would you rather stay here?"

"Shouldn't I see some of it, too?" asked the Countess. "Where are you thinking of going?"

"Nothing elaborate. Nothing even adventurous. I thought of taking a spin to Thysville and back. It's a day getting up there. We'd spend the next day there; we'd probably need to if bush travel is as arduous as it's reported to be. Show the face. Shake some hands. Return here the third day."

"Exhausted."

"Probably." The Count laughed. "Does it sound like something you couldn't miss?"

"Frankly, I can't imagine what I'd do here on my own. Settler women would undoubtedly want to take me under their wings." She gave an exaggerated shudder. The Count smiled. "I'm sure we oughtn't to be here if I feel like that. But I do."

"We'll go together then," said the Count. "I'll have Van Belle set it up."

"Will he accompany us?"

"I certainly hope so. I don't want to venture into the bush without someone who knows the territory."

Van Belle organized the excursion for the following fortnight. Leaving quite early in the day, he and the Governor-General and his wife boarded a barge that took them, the car they would travel in and its native driver east on the great river from Boma to Matadi, a river port town already becoming more important commercially than the capital.

Pleased by the prospect of a Governor-General's visit, local officials arranged festivities to honor him. School children and their mothers, government workers and men without work lined the streets as the Count and Countess were driven slowly through the town waving ceremonially as they made their way to the office of the territorial administrator. There they had tea and met European settlers.

From Matadi they drove on in the open car, the Lippenses in the rear, Van Belle and the driver up front. The sun was so fierce that the men were grateful for their pith helmets and the Countess for the broad-brimmed hat tied to her head by a scarf. Insects pestered them when they stopped. The car hurried along a track that led through country full of scrub growth with occasional tall trees. Off on the side of the track stood huts constructed of mud and wattle with occasional roofs of corrugated metal, but more often of thatch.

They saw women working at chores, babies tied to their backs, and men relaxing under heavily- and low-thatched structures without walls, open to the air; these seemed to serve as community centers. Tiny children, most of them naked, waved at the passing car. Older children ran beside it as if hoping to keep up with it.

The car, moving east, passed lines of natives headed west. The Count wondered if they were going to Nkamba. He wondered, too, if Kimbangu were out here, somewhere in the scrub country, healing and preaching.

The party reached Kimpese in time for lunch. The Count had written the British Reverend Larry Parkins to say they would be passing and would like to visit his mission station. On arriving there, the visitors were greeted by Parkins, his wife and staff, all well turned out. The Count realized, without surprise, that Parkins had made sure to have the station show its best face.

Even so, the station struck the visitors as a collection of old buildings – church, hospital, school, refectory, dormitory - rather in need of repair. The missionary homes gave evidence of occupants who cared little for material things. The furnishings were spare: hard, angular, locally made chairs in the parlors, tiny ascetic cot-beds pushed against an expanse of wall in the bedrooms. Although the bathroom was rude, every visitor was happy to take advantage of it. Keeping the station's buildings repaired obviously demanded time and labor that had nothing to do with spreading God's word.

Since the Count wanted to introduce reforms in the colonial education system, Reverend Parkins gave him a tour of the mission school. The two men discussed the problems of trying to educate children whose parents lacked any conception of European school learning.

The Parkins family offered the visitors a lunch that was simple in terms of repast, but lively in terms of conversation. They sat under a verandah of banana fronds, well protected from the sun, gentle breezes occasionally soothing them, and talked about the difficulties of fashioning a colony out of wild country and inhabitants unused to "better ways." The Count relished an opportunity to hear about the colony and its problems – "challenges," he preferred to call them – as seen from a perspective very different from that of Boma.

As they sat on the verandah, lunch concluded, drinking tea, the Count turned to Reverend Parkins and inquired, "May I ask a difficult question? One I think about frequently. One that must concern you."

Parkins smiled broadly. "I'm girding my loins, Governor-General. Go ahead."

The Count leaned back, gazing at the banana trees in the garden. "I am not being provocative. Let me assure you of that. But what is it that you are really doing out here?"

The reverend burst out laughing, so surprised was he by the question. He was also a bit taken aback.

"I thought maybe you could help me," explained the Count. "Because it's the question I ask myself time and again. Are we out here, trying to keep order so that we can more easily, more efficiently, divest the Congolese of the riches of this country? *Their* country. Congolese may not be aware of those riches. So it's not quite theft. Or is there another reason?"

"It is a difficult question," agreed Parkins. "I admire you for asking it."

"When you return home and do fund-raising. You visit churches?"

Parkins nodded. "And give talks."

"What do you tell the people when you ask for money?"

"You mean: How do we justify what we're doing?"

"Precisely," agreed the Count. "We have to justify ourselves as well. I wonder what you say."

"We generally show pictures of our station. Our activities. We explain that we are giving our Congolese education. And medical treatment. And helping them to live better lives by becoming Christians."

"And do people ask: For what purpose?" The Count leaned forward, his elbows resting on his knees. "Because that's what I keep asking myself. This is preparation, right?"

Parkins slowly nodded. The two wives looked from one speaker to the other, hearing questions articulated that they themselves often mulled, but never spoke about to their husbands.

"If it's preparation," the Count continued, then interrupting himself, asked: "Or is it? And if it is, it's preparation for what?" He spread his hands, his elbows fulcrums on his knees. "Look at my situation. I'll pester myself now, not you." The group laughed lightly, somewhat relieved. "I do under-stand the ideology to which we all genuflect: 'We rule in order to serve.' To serve Africa from which we are taking such riches. To serve Africans by bringing them what we call civilization. But I'm very aware that we're also serving ourselves rather well."

Again the spreading of his hands. "We tell ourselves we intend to educate these people, first mass education to create a literate population, to help form a middle class. Then eventually, beyond what we cannot even now imagine, we begin to form elites." The Count shook his head in bafflement. "But do we really want to educate these people? Do we want them to exchange their way of life for ours? What we should do with the best of motives, we often do with cruelty."

These remarks surprised the Count's listeners. Reluctant to consider them, they pushed back slightly in their chairs.

"I can't see the Congo becoming a province of Belgium," said the Count. "Can you?"

The others tittered.

"That's truly the tail wagging the dog. But if not that, what will it become? An independent nation?"

The group laughed.

The Count asked, "Should I consult some Congolese? Ask them where they see this headed?"

Parkins looked surprised. "They would have no idea what to say."

"Probably not," agreed the Count. He tried to explain. "But educated people want to rule themselves. They rather do that than have what we are prepared to give them: settled lives with reasonable housing, enough to eat and European spiritual resources. This leads to a contentious future."

"Ahh! The future!" sighed Mrs. Parkins with some relief. "And I keep wondering about getting through next week."

"I'm sure that's enough questioning," remarked the Countess, throwing her husband a glance that stressed, "Enough."

Not wishing to become a bore, the Count did not pose the questions that truly plagued him. If his efforts and the missionary's work actually provided Congolese with better lives, wouldn't those Congolese ask, "When do we get to govern ourselves?" For wasn't self-government an element of better lives? Yet if self-government seemed far-fetched, which it did, were the Belgians really here to dispossess the Congolese of their wealth? He did not want to be a part of that.

The talk moved to other subjects. Before long it was time for the Lippens party to push on. The Count found himself reluctant to leave. They lingered, knowing they would arrive in Thysville after dark.

Once they got back onto the track, they passed scrub growth again, a line of hills awaiting them outside Kimpese. "Goodness!" whispered the Countess to her husband. "Think of living that life."

"Did you find it so awful?"

The Countess shuddered.

"It was the bathroom, wasn't it? I was rather impressed."

"It was the talk, wasn't it? You found it refreshing, didn't you?"

In Thysville the Countess remained in the frontier-town hotel and read a book. The Count "showed the face," walking slowly through the town's main street, followed by an entourage of officials, waving to Africans who rushed to see him. At the town hall he had meetings and luncheon and was presented to settlers.

The day was long, but the travelers maintained their patience and good humor. The return leg of the trip, on the river again, offered fresh breezes and a glorious African sunset.

"Imagine doing all that on foot," said the Countess as they ate dinner. "That's how the Free State people did it thirty years ago."

"That excursion was worth our time," declared the Count, obviously refreshed by the outing. "I understand much more about the impact of Kimbangu on these people."

The Countess looked at him with surprise.

"You saw the monotony of those villages we passed," said the Count. "Those people have lived thereabouts forever. Year after year it's always the same. The rains come or don't. The crops grow or fail. Either way, always the same. Then suddenly everything changes. A prophet emerges. People don't have to die. Time may stop. No wonder everything's in upheaval. No wonder people have stopped working and are heading to Nkamba. I would never have gotten a sense of that staying in Boma."

THIRTEEN

A T THE SAME TIME COUNT LIPPENS WAS visiting Thysville, Léon-Georges Morel embarked on the quest Countess Lippens recommended to him. In fact, while Count Lippens walked along the main street of Thysville, Leon-Georges Morel stood before the mirror in the guesthouse in which he spent the night. He stood erect, threw back his shoulders, and smoothed his mustache. He considered himself a fine specimen of a colonial officer and set forth to call upon the Mother Superior of a convent school training sixty girls. He had set the appointment with another nun the previous day.

When he entered the office of this head nun, his heart sank. The woman sat behind her desk, swathed in her habit, her masculine face protruding from a wimple that looked a little the worse for wear. This was Africa, after all. The woman did not smile or rise in greeting to shake his hand. She studied him with narrowed eyes as if some magic had informed her of the reason for his visit.

He introduced himself, explained that he served as the territorial administrator at Cataracts-Sud, and observed that her convent school was extremely well-regarded in the area. The nun said nothing, continuing to study him. He said, "The Governor-General suggested that I call on you."

"Really?" she replied. Clearly she did not believe him. "And when did you see the Governor-General?" she asked.

Morel explained that he had been to Boma in regard to the prophet Simon Kimbangu.

"And why should the Governor-General suggest you call on me?"

Morel suddenly felt in greater danger than when he went to arrest Kimbangu. He hesitated, unable to mask his nervousness. "He recommended that I find a companion – the right kind of companion, of course, a girl with some education – and thought I might find her here."

The nun studied Morel. "You have come here to take off one of our best girls to keep you happy in the bush. Is that it?"

Morel felt tongue-tied.

"Does the Governor-General suppose we are doing our work to provide courtesans for colonial officers?"

Morel stared at the woman's forehead unable to meet her gaze. "I believe he feels that a gentle, docile girl with a sense of humor, rather pretty, would improve my ability to-- You know, deal with the challenges we face." Morel felt pleased with "the challenges we face."

"Less likely," said the nun, "to fly off the handle at natives, scream at them and beat them? Is that it?"

This was not going well. "Mother, it's a hard and lonely job. But a necessary one. A woman could—" Morel ran out of words.

The nun continued to examine him. "Hmm," she murmured at last. "We do have a girl, a complainer, rebellious, difficult to get along with. Rather plain. We were going to send her back to her village, but I suppose we could give her to you."

Morel watched the Mother Superior, terrified.

"Do you want to take her now?"

Morel shook his head. He could not speak.

"As for gentle, docile girls with a sense of humor, we hope to keep them for ourselves. To help us with our work." The nun watched him. "You understand, of course."

Morel stood, withering under the nun's scrutiny. He did not know how to extricate himself from the situation.

The nun rose from her chair and came around her desk. "I'll call the difficult girl. Perhaps you'd like a look."

"No, thank you," said Morel. He fled from the room as if his feet were on fire, stepped outside the building, relieved that he had escaped. He thought that there must be some better way to find a companion.

The evening after their return to Boma the Count faced hours shut up in his study with reports his absence had caused him to neglect. He must do the reading to stay abreast of his job. Although more tired than he realized, he proposed to his wife that they first walk down to the river for a bit of exercise. They went onto the porch. The Count lit himself a pipe. As they started down the stairs in the darkness, he turned to give his wife a hand. In doing so, he slipped. He fell down the stairs and gave a cry. The Countess rushed to him, holding the banister. "Are you hurt?" she asked. The Count grumbled, sought to make a joke of his clumsiness, reclaimed his pipe, and tried to rise. But he could not. The Countess helped him to his feet. She took his right arm to steady him. He winced.

"Darling, what is it?"

"The damn thing's throbbing. It may be broken."

Together they managed to regain the house. The Countess called the servants. They helped her escort the Governor-General to his study. Runners were sent for Van Belle and the town's best doctor.

When he arrived and had examined his patient, the doctor announced that the arm was broken. A clean break. It should heal rapidly. He adjusted the arm, put splints about it as a safeguard, and fashioned a sling in which the Count could rest it. There was no reason, the doctor declared, why he could not continue his normal duties. But he must avoid feeling stress; he must take things as easily as possible. He charged the Countess to be vigilant about making sure this advice was followed.

After the doctor left, the Governor-General said to his aide. "What a damned nuisance this is!" Van Belle studied him. "Speak to me, man. Tell me what you're thinking."

"I'm thinking, sir, that it's just as well this happened in the dark."

"Really? When I could hardly see my hand before my face?"

"When Congolese could not see you lying incapacitated on the stairs. Like a bird that's broken its wing and can't fly."

"Does this have something to do with the *chefferies*?" asked the Count.

"With Kimbangu," said Van Belle. He noted that the administration had twice attempted to engage Kimbangu, the second time to arrest him. He had foiled them both times. After hearing a report of the second attempt, the Count had fallen down the stairs of his residence and broken his arm.

"You're not proposing a connection between those things."

Van Belle shrugged.

"That's preposterous, old man."

"I don't claim there's a connection," Van Belle said. "In any case, what I think doesn't matter. But what will *they* think?"

The Count mulled this comment. "What do you advise?"

"Let's say nothing about this, sir. Carry on with your duties as usual. For the time being keep your contacts with Congolese at a minimum."

The Count studied his assistant. Finally he asked, "How long have you been out here, Van Belle?"

The assistant smiled. "Are you suggesting that it's too long?"

"I don't believe in magic," declared the Count. "Do you?"

Van Belle said, "I believe in being careful."

Count Lippens required some days to adjust to having a broken arm, a "wing in a sling," as he sometimes referred to it. He often changed position while sleeping and now frequently found himself awake in the night. His left hand rebelled at holding a pen. Writing with his right was possible, but not easy.

The left was also clumsy in using a fork; it seemed unable to bring the food directly to his mouth. This amused the Countess who lightly teased him. She began to make sure that he was served stews and casseroles, food he could manage. He tried not to appear in public, certainly not where he would be seen by Congolese. He just wished the damn thing would heal.

When young administrators visited the Count, they often inquired about his arm. The Count made light of it. The young men noted that in the tropics Europeans sometimes healed slowly. When they asked if the arm hurt, the Count said merely, "Not as much as Kimbangu."

Although he joked in this way, he gave little thought to the prophet. Or to the *chefferies*.

Or even to Sambry. In fact, one of the communications he read informed him that Sambry had been tried by a senior territorial administrator. This judge allowed testimony by Force Publique soldiers whose women Sambry had outraged to be entered into the trial's record. The administrator had sentenced Sambry to a year in a prison that usually housed Congolese. He was given time to exercise in the prison yard, but so many Congolese came to observe him that he spent most of his time in his cell.

The Count received petitions from settlers in several different locations objecting that a white man should not be treated in this way. Settlers visited his office in Boma with similar objections. The Governor-General listened to their complaints, agreed to consider them, but did not act on them. He also received a letter from a friend in Brussels warning him of whisperings in the palace. Those whisperings contended that the Count was lenient to blacks, but hard on whites. The friend advised him to take the whisperings seriously; there were hardliners in the Ministry of Colonies, holdovers from the Free State era, who could make trouble for him.

Occasional reports came that KImbangu was seen teaching here or preaching there. Most such reports arrived from the region of Bas-Congo. However, some came from as far away as Kinshasa where the prophet had once worked. The Count was content to have him preaching his version of Christianity in the bush. "Out there," as the Count thought of it, where he could not be found, particularly if the Force Publique did not look very hard for him. The prophet remained a problem very low on the list of priorities.

Of course, there were those who thought differently. Monsignor Van Rolse regularly visited the Count to complain that the administration was not sufficiently engaged in seeking Kimbangu. Planters sought audience to remind him that their workers had left the plantations to follow the prophet.

Count Lippens assured them all that their concerns were not forgotten. The more difficult the meetings, the more likely was his injured arm to throb. He often asked himself, "Why doesn't it heal?"

During these long weeks Countess Lippens grew increasingly concerned about her husband's health. She worried that the injured arm needed treatment it could not receive in Africa. She did not know that the arm occasionally throbbed while the Count sat in his office, especially during difficult meetings. Nor did she know that sometimes the Count stood before the fetish and asked, "What's going on here? Am I going to lose this arm?"

She did not realize that just as Morel's masculine identity seemed wrapped up in his mustache so was the Count's equanimity more and more dependent on his arm returning to full usefulness. However, whenever she proposed that he return to Europe for treatment, he refused to consider such a possibility.

Some evenings the Count took his coffee on the balcony overlooking the warehouses and shacks of Boma. He would hear drums from villages in one direction or another. The drumming made him wonder if Kimbangu were there. Was the drumming his way of thumbing his nose at administration authority?

One morning as the Count worked in his office, Van Belle knocked on his door and entered. The Count looked up to find his assistant grinning so expansively that he grinned himself.

"Here's something you won't believe, sir," Van Belle announced. "Simon Kimbangu has turned himself in."

The Count could hardly credit this turn of events.

"Truly," insisted Van Belle.

"How amazing!"

"It seems God told him to surrender."

"God did!" The Count stood. He reached out his left hand to shake hands with Van Belle.

"He's in our custody."

The Count went to the window and stood looking out at the river. He thought: Damn! Simon Kimbangu has just jumped well up the list of matters I must deal with. He turned toward Van Belle. "I would like to meet this man," he said. "Quietly, of course. Can that be arranged?"

"I'll see to it."

"In total secrecy." Van Belle nodded. "If the Monsignor forces the issue, I want to be able to tell him that the man has had my personal examination. And that it assures me that Kimbangu is not criminally insane." Then he added, "I suppose it's necessary to get this news to the palace in Brussels."

"It is, sir," said the assistant. "The palace is very interested in this matter."

After Van Belle withdrew, the Count stood before the portrait of Leopold II. "Did you hear that news, sovereign? Turned himself in. Did you make some recommendations to your contacts up there?" The Count laughed to himself, certain that Leopold did not have such contacts. He ambled over to the fetish. He took the measure of the sculpture and grumbled, "One thing more to deal with. If I had a nail and a hammer, I would pound a nail into your chest."

The Count returned to the window and looked out over the landscape. He had expressed a kind of exultation to Van Belle that Kimbangu was in the hands of the state. But, in fact, his moving about Bas-Congo, seemingly invisible, had suited the Count very well.

The present situation solved some problems, but created others. What was the state to do with him? How was it to regard him? Presumably he had sought a kind of protective custody. Was the state willing to honor that? And protection from what? Presumably assassination. But by whom? Congolese jealous of his notoriety and power? Or were there tribal machinations involved? Europeans never really could follow those. Or did he fear super-excited members of the Force Publique? Or an over-ambitious colonial officer eager to make a name for himself? Or betrayal by one of his lieutenants? That, the Count recalled, was what had happened to Jesus.

Kimbangu had apparently not had a trusted associate negotiate terms of his surrender. He had wanted to stop being a hunted man. Since that's what he was, it was easy for the state to regard him, once he surrendered, as a criminal. To lock him up in a cell.

But the Count did not consider him a criminal. He had committed no crime. This matter would have to be sorted out. Certainly if his administration intended to set the colony on a course different from the practices of the Free State era. The Count understood that most of his white brothers in the colony would want Kimbangu treated as a criminal. Jailed. And tried for sedition before a jury of white men who had suffered a very bad scare by Kimbangu's emergence as a prophet. The Count wondered: Could he stand in opposition to them? He thought again of the Free State era holdovers in the Ministry of Colonies. Experienced Governors-General, he thought, would know that treating Kimbangu fairly – like a European even if he was Congolese! - was not a matter to take a stand on. He wondered what he would do – or be forced to do.

FOURTEEN

NEWS QUICKLY SPREAD THROUGHOUT BAS-CONGO that Simon Kimbangu had surrendered to the state. The colonials were delighted. But there was sullenness in the villages. Count Lippens would stand on his balcony at night, listening to the drums, wondering what messages they sent.

Late one afternoon Van Belle received a note. He read it and presented it to the Governor-General. "The Baptist Reverend Parkins is in town and wishes to see you."

"Is it about Kimbangu?" the Count asked.

"Undoubtedly. He asks to come tomorrow morning."

The Count's arm began to throb. "My previous meetings with him were very pleasant," he admitted. "Have him come then."

The next morning when Reverend Parkins arrived at the State House, a young Congolese accompanied him. Guards refused the Congolese permission to enter the building. Reverend Parkins objected. He insisted that they had an appointment. His insistence fell on deaf ears. Patiently, but determinedly, he requested the Governor-General be informed of his arrival and his desire to bring the young man to the interview. Eventually a perplexed Van Belle came to the State House entrance. He conferred with the missionary and, despite Parkins's virtually unprecedented request, arranged for the young African to be allowed into the Governor-General's presence.

Once inside the Governor-General's office Reverend Parkins and Count Lippens exchanged pleasantries. The missionary noticed the Count's arm in a sling and inquired about it. The Count acknowledged that it was healing slowly. "It reminds me how new I am to Africa."

"When we met before," Parkins said, "you related a rumor about a man raising a woman from the dead. Simon Kimbangu?"

The Count acknowledged that it was he.

"He grew up in the BMS," said Parkins. "Our people trained him, baptized him. His uncle was one of our catechists. I don't know the man personally. But I'm sure he's a good fellow."

"You may know that Kimbangu surrendered to us voluntarily, wanting our protection."

"So I heard. I hear, too, that a lot of the colonials are insisting he be executed."

"Don't anticipate what may happen."

"I hope nothing drastic."

In answering, the Count chose his words carefully. "I admit there's a good deal of agitation for a trial. Kimbangu must have known that when he voluntarily put himself under the state's protection."

"How could he have known that?" Parkins challenged. "From what I understand he's done nothing wrong."

The Governor-General thought: My dear Reverend, I am committed to making sure that Kimbangu is not executed. But he made no reply.

"We both know where a trial's likely to lead," continued Reverend Parkins. Again the Count did not reply. "Surely there's nothing criminal about healing and preaching."

"Who's your young friend?" asked the Count, wanting to change the subject.

Parkins was happy to do that. "I brought him along," he said, "because when we met before, you wondered if you should consult Congolese. You may remember I was a little surprised." The Count nodded. "But now I have brought this fellow to you because he has a story to tell. I think you should hear it. I'll be happy to translate."

"Shall we hear it then?"

They turned to the young man. He began quite simply, "All my life I was a hunchback." The Count studied the young Congolese, perhaps sixteen; he stood straight before him. "My mother heard about a man at Nkamba who healed all kinds of disorders, the blind and the deaf. Some said he even restored the dead to life. We went to see him."

The Count wondered to what extent the young man had been schooled in telling his story. He did not look at the Count – perhaps that would seem impertinent - but he was very adept. He spoke without nervousness. The fact that he, a mere Congolese, was addressing the Governor-General himself seemed to cause him no self-consciousness. Probably he had related the experience many times over. The Count glanced at Reverend Parkins and offered a parental smile.

"Nkamba was full of people wanting to be healed," the young man continued. "I waited with the others. When it was my turn, my mother and I knelt before Simon Kimbangu. He placed a hand on my head. 'In the name of Jesus, stand up,' he commanded. 'Straighten your back and walk.'" At this point the young man looked at the Count. "I got up." He straightened his back in saying the words and smiled. "My back was straight; my hunchback was gone. I was healed and it didn't even hurt."

"Should you let the Governor-General see?" suggested Parkins. The young man removed his shirt so that the Governor-General could inspect his back. He handed the shirt to the missionary.

"I'm glad you're well," said the Count. "May you always be well." He patted the young man, a kind of congratulation, and took advantage of the moment to feel his back. It seemed perfectly normal.

"I know that this young man was hunchbacked from childhood," said Reverend Parkins, watching the Count's hand on the young man's back. "He is no longer. I can understand that you may not believe much of what you've heard about miracles. I do not believe it all myself." He returned the shirt to the young man who put it on. "Earlier when we met," said Reverend Parkins, "you kindly asked about my experiences. I thought perhaps you should hear this one."

"Thank you for coming," said the Count. He was careful in both his words and his manner not to reveal his skepticism about what he'd been told. He did that out of respect for Parkins' sincerity and long service.

"I can imagine the kind of pressure some of your people are putting on you," Reverend Parkins said. "I beg you: Don't let Kimbangu be harmed."

"I have not come here to harm Congolese," replied the Count.

"He has a gift of healing. It comes so rarely. It must not be snuffed out." Parkins looked deeply into the Count's eyes. The Count met his gaze. "And I thank you," the missionary concluded, "for seeing us and letting this young man tell his story."

After the visitors departed, the Count considered the account he had just heard. He realized Van Rolse could cite a dozen reasons why he should not believe it. But he was not prepared to disbelieve Reverend Parkins; the man had devoutly given his life to his work. Still he wondered about healing. Why – for whatever reason - had the young man's back become straight when his own arm refused to leave its sling?

He wondered how soon Van Rolse would learn of Parkins's visit. Did the guards at the State House entrance report who visited? The Count thought it a good thing to have a Congolese in his office. At times he felt caged. Before he left for lunch, he reminded Van Belle that he wanted a chance to talk with Simon Kimbangu.

At lunch he told his wife about the visitors he had received that morning. "Did you examine his back?" the Countess inquired.

"I put a fatherly hand on it. It felt like the back of our own sons."

"But it could be any child, couldn't it?"

"I assume that's what the Monsignor would think. And a lot of the settlers."

"Will 'His Holiness,'" she asked wickedly, "know you saw him?"

"Someone will tell him."

"Van Belle?"

"I hope not. A Congolese entering the State House was so remarkable an event that whispers of it have already risen to Heaven."

The Countess smiled. "Do you believe the young man's story?"

"No, I do not believe it," he said with conviction. "I could hear five hundred stories by people that Kimbangu has purportedly healed. They'd believe them, but I wouldn't." To avoid his wife's questioning look, the Count arranged his knife and fork on his plate so that the server would know that he had finished. His devout mother would believe it, he thought. His university training had taught him to be skeptical. But his ability to judge character, upon which his career had been built, told him to trust the missionary's sincerity. That was perplexing.

"True or not," he said, "there's no reason to harm Kimbangu. That's my real concern. Resist the settlers. You may not know it, but there's a pattern to these things."

The Countess frowned.

"In an environment like ours, the Count explained, "a healer, a prophet, arises. The people at the top of the pyramid are immediately frightened—"

"And become paranoid," said the Countess, finishing his thought. "They want to be sure that their little top-of-the-pyramid is protected. And they look to you to take care of things."

"But I'm determined not to take care of things in the way they'd prefer."

Buoyed by the good news of Kimbangu being in government hands, Léon-Georges Morel made a second attempt to secure a companion, this time at a Protestant mission training teenagers for Christian adulthood. Perhaps, he thought, a man would be more sympathetic to his quest. He was taken to the head missionary, an Englishman. His priggish reserve immediately alarmed Morel. When he heard Morel's request, he said, "Never before have I been mistaken for a procurer." Morel withdrew.

After two failures Morel's self-esteem hit bottom. His loneliness grew. His shattered self-confidence revived slowly. He felt a hunger, both sexual and spiritual, for a woman. He yearned for a companion to share his life, for someone to converse with at dinner.

One night, drinking with a trader spending the night at Cataracts-Sud, he recounted his encounter with the starchy prig of a deacon who probably had never had a woman. His interview with the ogre Mother Superior who needed a shave was even worse. He described her as a dog-faced hag with baboon-like incisor teeth that might bite off his nose. "She had a mustache," he said.

"As thick as yours?" inquired the trader, his words slurred with drink.

"My mustache becomes me!" insisted Morel. "Hers was—" He concentrated, then shouted, "Repugnant." At this moment, thoroughly inebriated, he could concoct no deeper insult . "She offered me a hellcat who might shrink my balls."

The two men chortled drunkenly at how impotent and awkward Morel had felt under the scrutiny of the Reverend Mother.

The next morning Morel's tender head vaguely remembered their laughter. The trader recalled enough of it to say that soon he would be visiting a convent school. He quite liked the Mother Superior there, a worldly woman, overcome by the world's sins, who had taken refuge from them in a religious calling.

"Let me sound her out for you," offered the trader. If she sympathized with a young man's bush loneliness, he would let Morel know.

As a result of Kimbangu's surrender to the authorities, a period of euphoria settled over the colonials in Boma. And, indeed, over all of Bas-Congo.

Monsignor Van Rolse made the point repeatedly in conversation and from the pulpit that Kimbangu had chosen not to fight against the whites and the civilizing mission they brought with them to Africa. By his surrender he endorsed the Europeans' higher mode of living. As proof, Kimbangu's loyal followers obeyed the precepts he taught: no lewd dancing, no fetishes, no polygamy, the very precepts missionaries had tried to inculcate from the time of their arrival.

On a visit to Boma Hans Bogaerts called on the Governor-General to report gratefully that his plantation workers were gradually returning from Nkamba. Many, he claimed, regarded Kimbangu's surrender as an acknowledgement that his mission meant to better, not to overturn, the lives that they were leading. His coming did not signal the end of time. As a result, it was a good thing to get back to the work that gave structure to their lives. The Count masked the skepticism with which he received this report; he jovially congratulated the planter on this upbeat turn of fortune.

The Monsignor told the Count that Congolese were returning to the One True Church. They were donating pittances once again at Sunday mass. The Count told him he could not be more pleased.

Judge DeRossi informed the Count that he was beginning preparations for a trial. The charge against Kimbangu would be sedition. The Count labeled such preparations premature. He pointed out to DeRossi that Kimbangu was under protective custody; his status had not yet been officially determined. General LeMoine assured the Governor-General that his troops remained ready to handle any emergency. The Count advised DeRossi and the general simply to enjoy the good times while they lasted.

The cathedral at Boma held a service of thanksgiving that Kimbangu was in the hands of the state. If the Count did not always attend mass, especially not with his arm in a sling, his wife insisted that on this occasion he must appear. He must be seen as grateful for the way events had unfolded. The Count donned his full Governor-General's uniform. He worshipped by the side of the Monsignor. Just before the service began, Van Belle told the Count, "I have set up your meeting with Kimbangu." The Count smiled and patted him on the back.

After the service Van Rolse welcomed him expansively. The churchman spoke of the Bas-Congo as having weathered a season of upheaval. The Count stood outside the cathedral and using his left hand shook hands with members of his staff, with territorial administrators who were present, with the commandant of the Force Publique detachment, with Judge DeRossi. "These are good days," DeRossi remarked to the Count. The Count nodded his agreement. "When I do try Kimbangu," he laughed, "I guess I can't let him off scot free. But I won't sentence him to be hanged from a yardarm by his thumbs."

At the service the Count endeavored to exude pleasure in the relief his fellow colonials were feeling. As they chattered about an upcoming trial, he let them misunderstand his position. He did not mention that he hoped to avoid a trial altogether and make other arrangements about Kimbangu that would satisfy the settlers.

However, when it came time to officially determine Kimbangu's status, the Count expressed his opinion that the man could not be tried; he had done no wrong. He realized immediately that the opinions of all his advisors were determinedly arrayed against him. Some argued that, indeed, he had done wrong. Others stressed that the colonial authority must show a stern face; it must assert its right to punish any Congolese who created public excitement.

When the Count pointed out that protective custody suggested not a criminal proceeding, but rather a special status, his opponents insisted there was no such thing, especially not for "natives." Moreover, Kimbangu had been on the run from arrest. That made him a suspect. Suspects who turned themselves in languished in cells like criminals, awaiting trial. When the Count opined once more that Kimbangu had committed no crime, his opponents asked why, then, had he taken flight. Furthermore, if he had committed no crimes, a trial would sustain his innocence.

When the Count suggested that Kimbangu be transferred from a jail cell and detained in a hospital, his opponents objected that no such facility existed, not even for colonials and certainly not for "natives." Moreover, the cost would be prohibitive.

The Count saw that his opponents were unanimously opposed to whatever he suggested. He wondered if some of the opposition was personal. Perhaps. Suspecting that, he realized that it would be a serious mistake to question the integrity of his advisers or to wonder about the impartiality of white men judging a black man. He did suggest that the fairness of the trial might be in doubt. This gave rise to personal criticism. "You've been here so short a time, Governor-General." "With a bit more experience, sir, you'd understand." He saw that his speaking too strongly for the prophet might poison relationships. It might damage his capacity to accomplish his goals and do nothing to help Kimbangu.

So he agreed to a trial. He insisted that a lawyer be found for Kimbangu, either a local man, if one was willing to do the job, or a defense attorney brought out from Europe.

FIFTEEN

ON THE MORNING THAT SIMON KIMBANGU WAS to visit him, the Count had his wife help him dress. She took special care with the sling that held his injured arm. As she did, he wondered: Why are we taking special care? The man was an African, a prisoner. He had caused innumerable problems.

A tension spread across the Count's chest. Why was that? What was he expecting to happen? He had not met many Congolese. A few chiefs.

The fellow Parkins had brought to him. The chiefs struck him as outlandish, otherworldly. He would not allow himself the word "savage." He was trying to expunge the term "native." He wondered: Would this man be different? Probably not. So why should he feel a tension?

At the office he moved back and forth between the portrait and the fetish, speaking aloud to neither. He wondered: What would Kimbangu think of him? What a strange thought! Could that possibly matter? Kimbangu was merely an African. But a special one. He felt a throb of pain from his arm. The injured arm. In the sling. The sling made him feel vulnerable. Another strange thought: Am I about to encounter the most interesting man I've ever met? Impossible. He had met kings.

A knock came at the door. The Count felt a catch of breath. Van Belle entered; he announced, "Simon Kimbangu is here. The guards have taken off the manacles."

"Give me a minute," requested the Count. "Then show him in."

Stand or sit? He had given that no thought. Standing would suggest a willingness to pay the prophet respect. Was that wise? But if he sat Kimbangu would look down at him. Could he allow that? He adjusted his arm in its sling. He grew quiet for a moment, preparing himself. Again a knock. He remained standing. He straightened up to his full height.

Van Belle entered. At his side walked a man who carried himself with dignity. "Simon Kimbangu, sir," said Van Belle. He turned to glance at the African, then gestured with his hand, "His Excellency Governor-General Maurice Count Lippens."

Kimbangu moved into the room walking with the steps of a man whose ankles had been manacled. He stopped. He measured the count with an expression that offered no challenge, no provocation. The men regarded one another.

The Count said nothing. His first reaction was to wonder why he had indulged himself earlier that morning with a fairy tale about this man being in some way distinguished. He was simply an African. There was nothing flamboyant, terrorist, or odd about him. He was of a bit more than medium height, rather stocky. Only moments before he had been wearing handcuffs and foot manacles. Now he stood erect, but not stiffly, in work pants and a tunic that came to his neck.

Strangely, as the two men studied one another, the Governor-General felt that, in fact, Kimbangu might be an authentic holy man. That idea startled him. Where had it come from? He had no idea what a holy man might look like. He knew, however, that if Kimbangu were an authentic holy man, they two would be equals.

It had not occurred to the Count that he might be meeting his equal. To take control of the moment, to assert his authority, he walked completely around Kimbangu, inspecting him from every angle. When he ended his circuit, he noticed that Kimbangu was staring with revulsion at the fetish.

The Count asked, "Why did you turn yourself in?"

"I did not want to be assassinated."

The Count had given no order for Kimbangu to be killed. Another question: "Did you think you could trust us?"

Kimbangu made no reply.

Finally the Count observed. "You have caused me a great deal of trouble."

The prophet smiled. "Sir, *you* have caused *me* a great deal of trouble." He glanced at the sculpture standing in the corner. "Why is that fetish in your office?" The Count made no reply. Kimbangu asked, "Do you pound nails into it?"

"I admire it as a work of art," the Count said.

"It wears a skirt."

"Its extravagant masculinity offends my wife."

"If it has power to offend your wife, think of its power for those who believe it possesses magic."

"It is wood and nails. It has no power."

"Wood and nails do not give it power. Superstition gives it power." Kimbangu stated this as a matter of fact, not as a provocation. The Count did not react. He continued to observe the prophet.

"It should not be here," said Kimbangu. Once more the remark was not meant to provoke the Count, merely to inform him. "We Christians are doing all we can to turn people away from fetishes. And you live with one."

The Count made no reply, then once more circled the visitor, inspecting him. Finally he said, "They say you talk to God."

Kimbangu smiled; he had heard this charge before. "God talks to me," he corrected. "I listen." As he measured the Count, Kimbangu's eyes softened. "You have great responsibilities," he said. "Does He not talk to you?"

The Count smiled at this inquiry, but made no reply. With patience Kimbangu waited for his interviewer to respond; there was no challenge in his manner. Finally he said, "He has a very loud voice." When Kimbangu said "He," there was no question to whom he referred.

The Count made no response.

Kimbangu raised his voice as if to illustrate his point. "It's *so loud* your head trembles when He speaks." Realizing the Count would not reply, he continued, "When He first spoke to me, I ran away."

A flicker of interest passed across the Count's eyes.

"To Kinshasa," explained the prophet. "I found employment as a domestic." The Count nodded ever so slightly. "Later I worked at an oil refinery." Kimbangu smiled rather sheepishly. "I was hiding. But God had no trouble finding me."

The Count cocked an eyebrow as if to ask why Kimbangu was hiding,

"I thought I might be insane."

The Count nodded.

"So I returned to the village of my birth."

"Nkamba,' said the Count.

Kimbangu smiled at the Count's honoring him with speech. "Yes." The men watched one another, Kimbangu outwaiting the Count.

"Did God instruct you to do that?" If there was scorn in the tone of the Count's question, there was even more genuine curiosity.

"On my way there I passed through a neighboring village. A woman on her deathbed cried out to me." Kimbangu regarded the Count with a look of genuine bafflement. "Why me?" He shrugged as if still unable to explain why the woman had chosen him. "I found myself approaching her." He gazed at the floor as if once again seeing the woman. He glanced up at the Count. "Unless I laid hands on her I knew that within the hour she would die."

He spoke as if urging the Count to share his dilemma. "I did not choose to approach her. I was told that I must do it." He glanced again at the floor as if beholding the woman. "There was expectation in her eyes." He looked back at the Count, mystified again. "Where did that come from?"

The Count listened without responding.

"I laid my hands on her shoulders." Kimbangu's arms moved forward, his hands outstretched. He brought the arms back against his body. He watched the Count intently as if his expression could make the explanation. "A strange influence came over me: the Holy Spirit. It possessed me. I heard holy voices shouting in my head."

The Count sensed a tension in the room. For just a moment Kimbangu's body stiffened, as if responding to some power outside it. "I began to tremble," he explained. The tension passed. His body relaxed.

The Count did not know what to think. He had not expected this.

"The woman sat up," Kimbangu said, still surprised at what had occurred. "She smiled at me. She stood." He looked at the Count as if wanting assurance that he understood the ambivalence he had felt. "I wanted to run. But I was still trembling."

Kimbangu spoke very quietly. He trembled. That caused a tightening along the Count's arms and across his chest. His instinct was to retreat. But he did not move. Kimbangu shook his head as if to throw off some confusion. "I could not run. I wondered if I were insane." He looked genuinely puzzled. "But how could I be insane if she was healed?"

He watched the Count as if truly hoping for some answer. The Count did not move.

"'The word was made flesh,'" Kimbangu said, his account of the incident ending. The trembling also stopped. "I knew that I could not run away from God any longer." The Count nodded. "I felt that He was pleased with me."

The Count turned his back as if to break a spell and removed himself several paces. "And the trouble began," he said.

Kimbangu smiled. "A woman was healed. How is there trouble in that?"

The Count ignored the question. "Tell me more."

"I went home," Kimbangu said. "People followed me. They crowded outside my domicile. I tried to ignore them." He gave a shrug as if to ask, "What could I do?"

The Count had grown tired of standing, but he would not sit while the visitor stood. He wondered if it were appropriate to invite a Congolese to sit. He could not remember ever seeing a Congolese seated in a white man's presence. "Should we sit down?" he suggested.

He moved to a pair of easy chairs before his desk and indicated for the prophet to take one of them. The prophet hesitated. The Count understood that Kimbangu could not imagine sitting with him. "It would please me if you would sit with me."

The Count sat. He watched the Congolese move to the empty chair and gingerly lower his body to the front edge of it. They looked at one another a long moment. "What was I saying?" Kimbangu asked.

"You said that crowds followed you."

"Yes," he said, remembering. "The sick came. For me to lay my hands on them." Kimbangu started to speak, but appeared uncertain of his perch on the front edge of the chair.

The Count said, "I think you will be more comfortable if you sit farther back as I am doing."

Kimbangu examined the Count's position in his chair and imitated it. He sat back, then leaned forward and spread his hands to explain. "The Spirit possessed me. I trembled and touched them and they were healed." The prophet watched the Count, seeking some indication that he believed him. The Count gave a small nod. "They began to say that an Mvuluzi had appeared to the Kongo people."

"An Mvu--?"

"An Mvuluzi: an apostle." The Count nodded. "They asked me to speak to them. I said merely what the Holy Spirit gave me to speak. That I was chosen to bring the Word of Nzambi to black people."

"Nzambi?"

"God," explained Kimbangu. "I said that Nzambi knew and loved them." He spoke with more conviction. "They did not need the intercession of white people to show Nzambi to the black people."

"And you believe that?" The Count asked the question as gently as possible, not as an inquisitor.

Kimbangu hesitated, as if his reply might have ramifications. "It was given to me to say," he answered carefully. He stood. He did not feel he could explain himself while he sat. The Count had an impulse to stand, but controlled it. He remained seated.

"I did not say I was Jesus Christ for the black people," Kimbangu explained. "Or the Second Coming. Others said that. Followers came."

The Count saw the puzzlement in the prophet's eyes. "They believed I had a power that I did not believe I had. They asked me to instruct them." The prophet spoke with more conviction now for he was not puzzled by how he had instructed them. "I told them to give up witchcraft. To stop evil dancing. To give up the drums. I told the men to marry only one woman. They obeyed me. These were the same things the Fathers and missionaries told them to do."

"I have heard of these things," the Count acknowledged.

"Suddenly other men arose. They claimed that they also were prophets, that they, too, had been visited by Nzambi in their dreams."

The prophet was speaking of the *n'gunza*. The Count offered no reaction, but listened carefully for it was from these men that political trouble would come. "They trembled as I had trembled in healing."

"Was their trembling genuine?"

"Of these new prophets I saw that some had truly been called by the Holy Spirit."

"How did you test them?"

"Others had not been called. Many are false prophets."

Of this, the Count was certain. "I am told they preach against the state."

"I have never preached against the state," Kimbangu asserted.

The Count rose and began to walk about the room. "The whites are sure there will be a rebellion," he said.

The prophet watched the Count and declared, "I preach obedience to the Bible. Against fetishes. Against alcohol. It is what the missionaries preach. My people do as I ask. That helps your people. This is not rebellion."

The Count turned toward Kimbangu. The atmosphere of their conversation had changed. The Count did not want to force the change, but needed to make some points with Kimbangu. "My people, who are so few among your people who are so many. . . They believe that your people mean to attack us."

Kimbangu stood his ground. "Our work is healing. We do as the Holy Spirit directs. We are not about killing."

"My people fear a black Christ."

"I never claimed to be Christ," insisted Kimbangu. "I am a messenger. There have always been prophets in Kongo." He now asked out of puzzlement, "For your people to be happy must all prophets be white?"

This question embarrassed the Count; he knew that the settlers would make that assumption. He moved to his desk, wanting to change the subject. "May I offer you something to drink?"

"I do not drink spirits."

"Water then?" suggested the Count. "There is a carafe of it here." The Count poured water into one of several glasses on a tray. He offered water to Kimbangu.

"Thank you, Governor. I need nothing." The Count continued to hold out the glass, assuming that after a perfunctory refusal the water would be accepted. "I know you will have to break any glass I use." The Count looked surprised. "No white man would ever drink out of it. I will take nothing."

This truth embarrassed the Count. For a moment he felt at a loss as to what to do. Kimbangu watched him with compassion. The Count set the glass aside and did not drink.

"I am sorry to see your arm in a sling," said the prophet. "A man must be careful going down stairs at night – even in his own residence."

The Count studied his visitor. His falling down the stairs had not been disclosed to the public. Ordinarily it would not be known to Africans. How would Kimbangu know this detail?

"You wonder how I know you fell," said Kimbangu, feeling ever more comfortable with the Governor-General. "As I approached the residence this morning, I saw you fall down the stairs. I am glad you were not hurt more seriously."

"The arm resists healing," the Count admitted. "No one knows why." He laughed with frustration. "The doctors have done what they can. A damned nuisance. The arm throbs sometimes. It is throbbing now."

Suddenly the Count found himself revealing something to this Congolese prophet that he had confessed to no one. "I fear that the arm will wither. I knew a German diplomat in Brussels who had a withered arm. It hung from his shoulder, useless." He shuddered, recollecting the diplomat. "I have dreams about that. It haunts me."

The two men gazed at each other. A realization of Kimbangu's purported capacities hovered between them. Neither man moved. At last Kimbangu stepped toward the Count, not subserviently as a black man before a white one, a prisoner before a governor. Gently he reached out and tenderly placed his hands on the Count's right arm. The Count grimaced, less in pain than in uncertainty.

Kimbangu closed his eyes, waiting for the Spirit to possess him. The Count watched him. Kimbangu began to tremble, unmistakably, but not violently. The Count witnessed the trembling. He felt a warmth flow into his arm. It increased.

Then it diminished.

Kimbangu stepped back, his eyes still closed. He stopped trembling. He removed his hands from the arm. He stood erect. He opened his eyes and beheld the Count. The Count shook his head.

At last the Count said, "Nothing happened." Kimbangu said nothing. "Why not?" The two men measured one another. The Count wondered what had disrupted the prophet. Why had the trembling stopped? Was it something in the office? The Count looked about. It could be nothing in the office. Kimbangu had not seemed thrown off before now. Then he thought: Of course. The prophet's capacity to heal was not so strong, after all. "What disrupted your trembling?"

Kimbangu said simply, "You did not expect to be healed."

The Count shook his head. Did the prophet mean that he had interfered with his own healing?

After a moment Kimbangu said, "That first woman, the one who called out to me, she expected to be healed." He smiled sadly. "The Holy Spirit will not give you something you do not want."

"But I want this!" cried the Count. "I want to be healed! Can you imagine what it's like having a withered arm?"

Kimbangu stepped away from the Count. "You would rather have a withered arm than to have a Congolese heal you. The people who came to me at Nkamba expected to be healed. Their spirit helps the Holy Spirit."

The Count turned away. He tried to take possession of himself, to mask the disappointment he felt. Had he truly prevented his own healing?

Kimbangu watched him gain control of himself. He asked, "What will the administration of the Belgian Congo do to me now that I have turned myself in?"

The Count turned back to face him. "I find you did no wrong," he said. "But there will be a revolt among the settlers if nothing is done. My people are afraid. They insist that you be put on trial."

"Under what charge?"

"Sedition." There had been a moment of connection between the two men. Now it was gone. They were talking business. "Preaching rebellion against the state."

"I have never preached against the state."

"Disturbing public tranquility." The Count softened his tone. "You have given the whites a bad scare."

"And how will they punish me?"

"There will be a trial. The judge will determine." The Count felt that this was not a satisfactory answer. The man deserved better. "I hope a lawyer will represent you." Kimbangu looked uncertain about this. "I assume the punishment will be imprisonment in a penal colony. Far from here."

Kimbangu said, "Some of your people want to see me executed,"

"I don't deny that." The Count spoke more kindly. "Imprisonment long enough to let things cool down." He shrugged. "Maybe. . . Five years."

Kimbangu heard the words without emotion. Finally he said, "Thank you for seeing me. For allowing me to sit in your presence. For offering me water."

"I wish we were meeting in different circumstances." The Count reached out his free left hand in a fellowship he would not have thought possible when the visitor entered the office.

Kimbangu took the offered hand in his right hand. The two men looked at one another. Count Lippens started to tremble. His eyes widened in alarm. Warmth infused his injured arm. Kimbangu clasped his free hand over the hand holding the Count. The Count's trembling increased to a shaking. The room became filled with brilliant light of a kind the Count had never before witnessed. Kimbangu began to tremble, less violently than the Count. The two men held one another. The Count's right arm began to move forward out of the sling. The Count's eyes grew wider. His mouth opened involuntarily. Kimbangu held on to him more firmly. The light grew even brighter and the Count's right arm moved out of the sling.

Once it was free of the sling, the Count pumped the arm. He rotated it. He shook it. He looked uncomprehendingly at Kimbangu. The prophet smiled at him through the great light. The Count placed his newly freed hand over Kimbangu's. Tears flooded into his eyes. He began to weep. He shook Kimbangu's hand, then released it and turned his back to hide his emotion.

Kimbangu watched for a moment. Then he left the office.

Count Lippens fell to his knees. As the light continued to shine, he wept with relief and gratitude.

When Van Belle entered the Governor General's office, he found the Count sitting at his desk, staring meditatively before him. The Count still felt the warmth in his arm, but the brilliant light had begun to fade. Even so, glancing around the office, Van Belle grew aware of an unusual brightness. He felt that Kimbangu had left the Governor's office in an unexpected manner. Had something happened there? Perhaps he should check with the Count. "Is everything all right, sir?" he asked. "Did that go as you'd hoped?"

"Yes." The Count did not look at him. "Better, in fact. All the Governor-Generals who ever served here never had an encounter quite like that."

Van Belle noticed that the Count's right arm no longer rested in the sling. He saw a piece of cloth over the back of an easy chair. Was that the sling? He glanced again about the room, peered out the window. The room did seem brighter than the sun would light it. He wondered what had happened, but he did not ask.

And the Count did not explain. Still staring meditatively before him, he suggested, "Could you arrange for the residence to send over some soup for my lunch? I will stay here the rest of the day."

"Of course." Saying no more, Van Belle withdrew.

For a long time the Count sat, pondering, manipulating his right arm which he had not done for many days. It had never occurred to him that he would witness the presence of the Holy Spirit. But how else could he explain the brilliant light? Nor had it ever occurred to the Count that the Holy Spirit could act on him. He would not have thought it possible that such a spirit could possess him, that he would tremble uncontrollably, that he would feel a black man's tender touch on his arm, that healing warmth could bloom in his bones, that light could shine with such brilliance. Sitting at his desk he rotated his arm. No, it was not an illusion. The arm was healed.

The Count was not superstitious. He did not believe in miracles. He would simply call what happened "spirituality manifest." He was not religious, but he did believe in spirituality.

When his arm did not heal, he had known a genuine fear that it would wither. Dreams of a withered arm had disturbed his sleep. He kept remembering the German diplomat he had known in Brussels. When his arm was restored, the Count wept with gratitude. That emotion remained with him; he feared that tears would flow again if he spoke of the healing to anyone. So he resolved to remain in his office the rest of the day, trying to come to grips with what had happened to him.

The Count sat at his desk, turning a fountain pen over and over in his fingers. He wondered: Would this healing leave him where it found him? Or would he now become a different person? A better person? But what did that mean? Was he not already trying to do a difficult job in a sane, rational, and humane way? More importantly, did the healing alter his relationship to the healer? Did it make moral demands on him?

He was now convinced that Simon Kimbangu was an authentic holy man. Of deep spirituality. Did Kimbangu expect to get some quid quo pro for the healing he had worked? The Count did not think so. Kimbangu healed because it was what he did. It was his art and he expressed his art.

He himself was a civil servant, a colonial administrator in a job replete with political ramifications. He wondered: had Kimbangu's healing him placed him in a position of moral compromise? That had not been Kimbangu's intention; of that he felt certain. Kimbangu healed because that was his nature. But must he, Maurice Count Lippens, be involved in the troubled destiny that awaited Kimbangu in this colony? Could he, Governor-General, block or thwart that destiny?

SIXTEEN

THE COUNTESS ACCOMPANIED THE SERVANT who brought the Count's soup from the residence. When she saw that his right arm was no longer in the sling, she looked concerned. As soon as the servant withdrew, she went to her husband. She stood close to him, her hands on his, and peered deeply at him. "Are you all right?" she asked. "You have never asked to have food brought to you here." Before he could answer, she added, "Why is your arm out of the sling?"

The Count looked at her very strangely and suddenly began to weep. She knelt beside him. "Darling, what is it?"

When the Count got control of his emotion, he explained what had happened: the trembling, the warmth, the light. Hearing what had occurred, the Countess burst into smiles. "Is it true?" she asked. "Is it healed?" The Count put his right arm around her, brought her to him, patted her bottom with his healthy right hand, and kissed her. She began to weep and, weeping, laughed joyously with her husband.

In time she pulled out of his embrace, went to the desk, and arranged soup for both of them. As they ate, the Countess said, "I see. This is now delicate for you. How can you possibly let them—" Her words hung in the air.

"They mean to try him for sedition."

"You can't—"

He shook his head. "In a sense the judgment has already been rendered. They want him executed."

"You can't obstruct that?"

"I will try, of course. I will tell anyone who asks: 'Do not expect me to execute an innocent man while I am Governor-General.' I will say that, but I cannot commute. Brussels has taken an interest in this matter. If anyone commutes, it will be the palace."

The Count discussed the matter at length with his wife. When she left him, he wrote out a list of options for action. He did not like what he wrote.

Toward the end of the day he spoke with Van Belle.

"It's wonderful that your arm is healed," said his assistant.

"But it creates difficulties."

I'm afraid it does." Van Belle admitted that he had discerned the healing

126

earlier in the day. He had been wrestling with its meaning ever since. "It would be best not to acknowledge Kimbangu's role in this healing," he advised.

"Have you been reading Machiavelli?"

"Just imagine what the Congolese would do with this. The Governor-General healed by the prophet's magic!"

"It was not magic," the Count declared firmly. "It was" – he shrugged – "spirituality."

Van Belle who had spent so many years in Africa made no reply.

The Count measured him carefully. "Assure me that you do not believe it was magic."

The aide shrugged. "I'm not sure what it was."

The Count laughed and used his right arm to slap Van Belle on the back. "You trained for the priesthood. And you cannot recognize spirituality when it comes knocking at your door?"

Van Belle stepped beyond the reach of the ebullient arm. "The important thing is: What will *they* think? You can tell them spirituality. They will understand that to mean magic. The bush telegraph will spread the word of this healing all over Africa."

"Brussels will think I've gone native, consulted a witch doctor," remarked the Count. He laughed as if at a joke he had told, then stated an idea that struck him as preposterous. "My usefulness may be at an end."

Van Belle smiled, too. He agreed, "Yes." But he did not laugh. Finally he said, "The settlers will insist that Kimbangu be hanged." He added sadly, "And he will be."

The Count said quietly, "That will not happen."

After Van Belle withdrew, the Count pondered the future. After nightfall he returned to the residence. Darkness hid the fact that his right arm no longer rested in a sling.

The Count and his wife discussed ramifications of the healing at dinner. By the time he went to bed, the Count had decided that to deserve Kimbangu's gift of healing he must deal with the political consequences of it as best he could. He must be the best Governor-General he knew how to be. But it was not clear exactly what that would mean.

In the days immediately following Kimbangu's visit, the Count felt changed. The brilliant light that shone so brightly did not shine again. The warmth he had felt throughout his body did not return. But he felt that the healing had transformed him. It made him consider carefully his responsibilities as Governor-General. In the past he had thought, I will save this man from whatever schemes the church and the settlers have to destroy him; I have a moral obligation to prevent the taking of innocent life. But now his commitment to protecting Kimbangu was deeper. It was unthinkable to consider extinguishing a healer.

And yet Kimbangu was in the hands of the state. Settlers believed that he was a menace to their tranquility. And so he must be tried. The colonial authority must still assert its right to punish any Congolese who created public excitement.

Count Lippens felt certain that no credible case could be made against Kimbangu. The settlers did not agree with him. He was not even sure that Van Belle agreed with him. The settlers meant to have Kimbangu executed to placate their paranoia.

The work of reordering the *chefferies* continued. The Count tried to attend to it. But underneath that effort, he kept turning over in his mind ways to alter Kimbangu's destiny. He came up with a plan.

One afternoon he decided to test it on Van Belle. He called the assistant into his office. "I have a matter I want to discuss with you," he said. Van Belle stood attentively beside his desk. "Please have a seat," invited the Count, gesturing to chairs on the opposite side of the desk.

Van Belle seemed surprised at this instruction, closed the door, and took a chair. "This sounds serious," he commented.

"Yes," agreed the Governor-General. Once his assistant was seated, the Count rose and began meditatively to walk about the office, his hands clasped behind his back. "Kimbangu surrendered to us voluntarily," he said. He stopped, turned squarely toward Van Belle, and made his proposal. "What if we offered him a release plan?"

Van Belle did not know how to react. The notion was unthinkable. He realized, however, that the Count had been mulling it for days. "There would be a terrible uproar about that," he remarked carefully. His role was to help the Count think out ideas; he would see what he had in mind.

"I am willing to face that," said the Count.

Van Belle did not at first reply. Finally he offered, "The settlers would be furious. They might demand you be recalled"

"And I could face that," remarked the Count mildly. He resumed pacing, walking back and forth close to the nail fetish. "It would be done secretly. The settlers needn't hear of it until after it was carried out."

Van Belle watched him move and said nothing.

"When the time came," said the Count, "I believe we could give an adequate justification."

"Which would be?" Van Belle rose from his chair and began also to walk about, choosing to move under the watchful eye of Leopold II.

"Our position would be that the state has no credible charge to make against him. Any serious charge of sedition is laughable." The Count continued to walk. "We would stress that Kimbangu did not surrender to us. Rather he sought our protection." Van Belle stopped pacing and watched the Count. "We would contend that protection did not legally involve imprisonment. Therefore imprisonment cannot be justified." The Count stopped walking and tried to assess his assistant's reaction. He continued, "I am concerned that our custody of Kimbangu be regarded as imprisonment. That if there is a trial, that suggests the colony has a right to execute."

"Have you discussed these legal matters with DeRossi?"

"No. You're the first person to hear of this." He started walking again. "DeRossi believes the state can do whatever it wishes. Legal justifications can be concocted after the fact."

He stopped walking and looked at Van Belle. Van Belle said nothing.

He started walking again. "I am afraid the settlers will demand the death penalty. To appease their paranoia." The Count confessed, "I have made a commitment to myself that no innocent man will be executed while I am Governor-General."

Van Belle absorbed this news without speaking.

The Count lowered his voice. "This is confidential. I am concerned that Judge DeRossi lackS the backbone to sentence according to the evidence."

Van Belle folded his arms across his chest. "What kind of a release plan? What do you have in mind?"

"It's not total release," the Count assured his subordinate. "We would offer Kimbangu transfer to a distant location."

"Where he would remain under our protective custody?" asked Van Belle. "Which is not to be confused with imprisonment."

The Count smiled. "Something like that." He took more steps around the office as he outlined his plan. "There he'd be under a kind of generous house arrest." Steps. "He'd be able to wander locally under the state's watchful eye." More steps. "But not to heal or preach."

"Rustication."

"A generous rustication." The Count looked squarely at Van Belle. "Obviously what I am trying to do is put him beyond the reach of execution."

Van Belle shrugged.

"He came to us because he feared assassination. So he's undoubtedly interested in saving his life." The Count resumed pacing. He explained, "We'd place him where few people had heard of him."

Van Belle began to think that maybe such a plan could work. "For how long?"

"No more than five years." The Count moved back across the office, away from the fetish into the sphere of influence of the portrait. "Maybe less if the furor calms down." The Count sat at his desk, put his hands on top of it, and folded them.

Van Belle returned to his chair, sat, and asked, "Where would you place him?"

"You know the colony better than I do. A location well away from here. Large enough for us to keep an eye on him. Anything strike you?"

Van Belle peered at the floor, imagined a map of the colony there, and quickly moved his eyes across it. "Stanleyville in the center of the colony," he suggested. "Or Costermansville on the eastern frontier. But both those are difficult to get to; it would not be easy to transfer him secretly to either one. Perhaps Coquilhatville would be suitable," he concluded. "It's a river port in the Equateur, the province's principal town. He could be transferred there easily and secretly by boat. Territorial officers there could monitor him." The Governor-General nodded. The two men mulled the possibilities.

Finally Van Belle asked, "How would you actually handle this 'release'?"

"We will call it a 'transfer,'" said the Count. "The term release could cause us endless trouble."

The Count explained, "It would be an operation of the highest secrecy. We'd set up the receiving end first. Find colonial officers who can keep their mouths shut. Get a house for him near the town, but not in it. Then we'd begin the transfer in a closed vehicle after dark."

"On a ship obviously on the river," commented Van Belle. The Count nodded. "Boma to Coquilhatville could take as long as a week."

The Count smiled. "No hurry," he said. "Everything done in secret."

"Secrets travel in this place," observed Van Belle.

The Count shrugged. "We keep the transfer secret as long as possible."

"That won't be long. There'll be settler agitation."

"Once he's there, maybe we release the news of the transfer – without fanfare. Or maybe not. We'd keep the location secret."

Van Belle rose again and moved around the office. The Count watched him, no longer feeling the need to pace. "Would you tell the palace?" Van Belle asked.

"Only after it's done," the Count said. "A fait accompli. If there are objections, I might tell the palace that, while I'm Governor-General, I'm unwilling to have this innocent man executed."

"The palace might deem that too independent."

The Count shrugged.

"How does your plan work in Boma?"

"We'd need trustworthy men to help us transfer him to the boat. Are there a dozen men in Boma who can keep a secret?"

"Certainly no more than that," said Van Belle. "How would you justify this to the settlers once they realize he's been moved?"

"We'd say he's in protective custody in an undisclosed location. To keep him safe from people who want to do him harm." He continued, "I would explain to Brussels that this seemed the best way to avoid bloodshed in Boma."

"Would Brussels believe there might be bloodshed here?"

"We'd have to find out."

Having unfolded the release plan, the Count felt a certain confidence that it could solve the Kimbangu problem.

"And you think the settlers could be appeased?" said Van Belle. "Frankly, I'm skeptical."

"We'd have to see."

"If they can't be appeased, you might be recalled."

The Count shrugged.

"You're willing to jeopardize all the reforms you've started here because of this?"

The Count said, "I am."

Van Belle thought that an attitude like that came from belonging to the nobility. A mere mortal could not take that risk, but a nobleman might get away with it. "If I may," he said, "let me suggest how the palace will look at this notion, given its sensitivity to settler feeling."

The Count nodded his head, signaling the assistant to continue.

"It might say, 'Kimbangu is only one Congolese. Many men have died so that Belgium could build a colony in Africa. Why risk exciting the settlers over one Congolese? Especially when people we trust – like Van Rolse – tell us he's a danger to the community?"

The Count replied, "Not while I'm Governor-General. I am trying to set a new course from what was done in the Free State era."

Van Belle nodded, willing to consider the plan – at least for the moment. He rose and stepped away from the Count's desk. "I can't serve you well, sir, if I don't tell you this: I think the plan is foolhardy."

"Then come up with something better that rescues Kimbangu." After a moment the Count asked, "Who could propose this arrangement to Kimbangu?" He added, "I'm not the right messenger."

Van Belle commented, "If secrecy is necessary—"

"And it is," added the Count.

There was a moment of hesitation. They two alone had discussed the plan. Was it wise to bring in a third person? Van Belle thought not. "I suppose it has to be me," he acknowledged.

"Yes," agreed the Count, studying him. "But you must believe wholeheartedly that it's the best way for us to proceed. You cannot convince Kimbangu unless you believe totally in the plan."

Finally Van Belle said, "I can see that it's the best plan for Kimbangu. We'll have saved his life." He added, "However, I'm uncertain that it's the best plan for us."

The Count continued to study his assistant. Clearly the young man did not believe that the plan would succeed. But the Count trusted that he would not maliciously undermine its presentation. Finally he nodded and instructed, "Make the proposal to Kimbangu and let me know his reaction."

SEVENTEEN

THE MATTER OF THE AFRICAN PROPHET DID not disturb the Governor-General for several days. Then Van Belle entered his office and said, "I have met with Kimbangu."

The Count looked up, immediately interested. "And?" he queried.

"I met him in a private conference room."

"Was he manacled?"

"Outside his cell he is always manacled. Unless he comes to see you."

The Count shook his head. ""What a way to treat a holy man."

"I presented the proposal," Van Belle continued. "I showed him where Coquilhatville was located and explained that the proposal was made to safeguard his life. He asked for fifteen minutes to pray."

"He needed to talk to God."

"Apparently. I left the conference room. When I returned, Kimbangu said that God had advised him not to agree to our proposal."

The Count allowed his expression to show his disappointment. "Does he not trust us?" He could not believe, given the rapport they felt at the time of the healing of his arm, that trust was the problem.

"Perhaps not," Van Belle said, knowing that this would distress the Count. He added, "Nor does his God."

"Does he understand that if he remains in our custody, there will certainly be a trial?"

"I made that clear to him." The Count wondered if the problem was Van Belle's trust. Had he lost confidence in the plan? That it could be carried through? He wondered how effectively Van Belle had actually presented the plan. "It occurred to me," continued the assistant, "that he believes God has given him a calling. If he agrees not to preach or heal, he may be betraying it."

Yes, thought the Count, he may believe that our prohibiting his preaching and healing amounts to a kind of execution. He considered this probability for several moments. Then he said, "Thank you, Van Belle. Let me give some thought to what comes next."

After Van Belle withdrew, the Count wondered if he should meet with Kimbangu. But he realized that was impossible. Word of such a meeting would sweep through the settler community. Van Rolse would be knocking at his office door immediately.

The Count began to worry about the likelihood of Simon Kimbangu standing trial. Traditionally the Governor-General had jurisdiction over the judicial proceedings of the colonial government. But in the matter of Simon
Kimbangu, the Ministry of Colonies and the palace in Brussels requested
jurisdiction. Given his disagreements with the Ministry, the Count knew that
he must keep hands off.

Still, he was concerned about the manner in which Amadeo DeRossi was
preparing for a trial. The Count had no confidence in the man. He doubted
that he would conduct a trial fairly. He was troubled that DeRossi could not
conceive that the prophet deserved a proceeding as fair as any accorded a
white man. He was bothered by the likelihood that DeRossi could convince
himself that any proceeding was fair – or as fair as a mere Congolese deserved.
He understood that DeRossi would take umbrage if the Governor-General
even hinted that the proceeding was a show trial, a public event intended to
appease settler opinion, to serve as a warning to Congolese, and to obscure
the predetermined outcome.

Both the Count and DeRossi were seeking a defense counsel for Kimbangu. When the Count suggested that the trial be postponed until an
attorney was found, DeRossi insisted on going ahead. "The settlers and
the palace wonder why we are delaying," DeRossi complained. The Count
could not overrule his decision to proceed. When the Count objected to
the charge of sedition, DeRossi very cautiously said, "My dear Count, this
matter is out of your hands." And so Kimbangu would be found guilty of
sedition, although the evidence of that sedition existed only in the minds
of settlers.

The Count felt strongly that separation of powers was an important pre-
cept. He wanted to strengthen it. But the trial was an exception. He spent
many hours pacing his office, wondering what he could do to further the
possibility of a fair proceeding.

While the Count worried about a trial, another trader passing through Cataracts-Sud stopped by the office of Léon-Georges Morel and handed him a
letter. "You're the chap looking for a slim, pretty, good-humored companion,
right?" said the man. "I think there's good news here for you."

Indeed there was. The Mother Superior with experience of the world
understood the pain of loneliness and the calls of the flesh. She invited Morel
to visit her school.

He immediately made arrangements to journey to that part of the region.
When he appeared before this woman, he found an entirely different person

from the first Mother Superior he had confronted. Like her sister nun, she peered at him from out of a wimple, but in her former life she had had experience with men. The pleasure of beholding a fine-looking young fellow made her smile. Her eyes sparkled. "The colonial service has a number of handsome officers in it," she enthused. "I think any number of our young ladies would be happy to be a companion to you."

"What good news," said Morel. "Thank you!"

The Mother Superior had, in fact, identified five candidates, fifteen or sixteen years old. They were all rather pretty. "Some African girls are really stunning, you know," confided this gentlewoman. They also had pleasing personalities. She suggested that Morel have tea with each candidate. She would introduce them, make sure some rapport was established, then discreetly depart.

She suggested that Morel see one girl in the morning and another in the afternoon. When he had seen them all, he could make his choice. At that point the Mother Superior would undertake negotiations with the family of the chosen girl. Morel knew that he would have to pay her father bridewealth. He told his new friend what he could afford.

"The girl and her family will understand that this is not a marriage," the Mother Superior explained, laying out the details. "But the girl will be pleased to be a white man's woman. That means she will be prized. When the time comes for you to leave her, she will have no trouble finding a husband, particularly if she gives you a child."

Morel's eyes grew large at this remark. He had not thought of him and the companion producing children.

"In the old days before we civilizers came out here," said the nun, "there was a kind of rental relationship between a man and a woman. Fortunately, those are less frequent now, but this is somewhat like those. You must understand that, if the girl has a child, that child belongs to her lineage. You'll have no rights to it." The nun looked at Morel sympathetically. He nodded his agreement to this stipulation. "A man can become very attached to his children," noted the Mother Superior. "But if you wanted to leave her, you would have to give up the child. To keep the child you would have to marry her."

"I understand," said Morel. He was eager to begin the round of teas.

"If you want, you may ask them to shed their clothes," continued the Mother Superior. "Africans are more modest than we generally are," noted the nun. "Some will be very reluctant to remove their clothes. But they will oblige you. Some may have scarification designs on their backs. You will want to check on that." The woman hesitated, then counseled. "During these teas it would not be appropriate for you to have relations with any of them." She smiled apologetically. "While they are at our school, we encourage them not to know men."

"I understand," Morel said again.

The teas began. Morel felt enthusiastic about the process. Young girls were paraded before him to audition for the role of his companion. The ceremony of tea allowed him to assess their manners, their training, their language skills, their ease or lack of it in being with him. All of the girls were both friendly and pretty; one was striking, a beauty. Morel was pleased at the idea of beholding beauty every day.

Some girls were shy about conversing; his friend helped bolster their confidence. Morel tried humor, teasing, flirtation with all of them. Some remained relaxed when his sponsor left them alone; others allowed shyness to return. Morel did not ask any of the girls to shed their clothes, except the beauty. Her back was clear of scarification designs. When the girl stood before him naked, Morel's throat went dry. He felt breathless, dizzy.

He chose the beautiful girl who had stood before him unclothed. The nun was not surprised. Men were men, after all. She would not announce the choice to the girl until she had negotiated with her family. As it turned out, the beautiful girl's father would not agree to the arrangement. He expected to make a marriage for her within the next year and anticipated receiving more bridewealth than Morel could afford.

Morel once again felt discouraged. He had pinned all his hopes on winning the beauty. "I suspected you would make that choice," the Mother Superior told him. "But personally I think it was the wrong one. Living with a woman who is conscious of her beauty is not an easy road. Her father may have done you a good turn."

"Which one would you have chosen?" asked Morel.

"You and Titi had the most rapport. I thought it was a match."

So Morel chose Titi. She was sixteen, pretty, with a lively personality, gentle but not docile, with a dark skin and laughing eyes. Her family was agreeable to the arrangement. Morel had tea with her again – they were alone - and told her he had chosen her. She seemed pleased and laughed. She took her clothes off with little urging and walked about the room, waving her arms, pleased with both herself and him. Watching her, Morel's mouth watered.

Titi had little French. Their conversations would progress slowly. However, she touched his mustache with delight, this special secret of white men. They had another mystery about them: their skin. Titi grasped Morel's arm.

She pinched him. She spit into her hand and rubbed his skin. The white did not come off; it was not ashes as whiteness was in her village.

Titi communicated that she expected Morel to show her his body.

"What?" Morel asked, surprised.

"Off!" she said, laughing at him. "*Tout nu.*" Teasing, Titi began to tug at his clothes. When she opened his tunic, she reacted with surprise. His chest was covered with hair. European men were hirsute; African men were not. She reached out to touch the nest of hair. She pulled at it. Morel gently pushed her away, offended. They stared at one another.

Titi signaled him to continue removing his clothes. He meant to have her and complied. Soon he was totally naked. Titi discovered he was completely white. To overcome his self-consciousness at being stared at, he walked around the room as she had, waving his arms and strutting. They laughed at each other. He felt himself growing erect and covered his groin.

When Morel stopped, his hands linked before him, Titi made an inspection. She moved completely around him and finally nodded her approval, willing to give their arrangement a try. One final test. She reached out to his face, seized his mustache and ruffled her fingers through it. Pleased with it, she accepted him.

The next day Morel met Titi's parents and transferred the bridewealth to her father. Titi left the convent school that afternoon and went with Morel to the guesthouse.

It did not bother Morel that she seemed to have had some experience with men. After first being together, they sat on their bed, she on his knees, *tout nu,* laughing and kissing, shaking their heads in bafflement as they exchanged incomprehensible words. Morel rested his hands on her hips; Titi once again examined his mustache, flicking its long points back and forth, laughing heartily and whispering, "*Si beau! Si beau!*"

When he lay beside her that night, his arms about her, his body sated, a grin on his face, Morel felt a satisfaction he had not known for many months.

As the days passed, the inevitability of Kimbangu's trial deeply worried Count Lippens. He wrote to progressive lawyer acquaintances in the metropole, seeking someone willing to defend the prophet. The ablest of them were too busy to spend weeks journeying to the colony in an effort that struck them as undoubtedly futile. Others, swayed by photographs they had seen of Congolese depicted as savages, could not be persuaded that Kimbangu deserved their representation. No help came from the metropole.

The Count tried to find a local counsel. But no lawyer in the colony would take the case.

The Count passed troubled weeks. He watched impotently as the process of Kimbangu's trial inexorably moved forward.

The Count and his wife did not ordinarily hold one another at night except when they had made love. But in this difficult time the Count reached out for her support, holding her, even when he was awake, mulling his options. The couple did not make love during this period; circumstances were too turbulent for the Count to feel sexual. But he clung to his wife almost every night.

EIGHTEEN

Finally Count Lippens determined that he must see Amadeo DeRossi. He sent the judge a note, but not by Van Belle whom he did not want involved in any negotiations. He sent it by one of the men at the residence, saying that he would call on the judge. He did not tell Van Belle where he was going; Van Belle did not need to know. He met the judge in what passed as DeRossi's chambers. DeRossi offered the Count a glass of sherry and they began their consultation.

"I am sure you have given a great deal of thought to this matter of Kimbangu," the Count began. "So have I."

DeRossi rubbed his nose meditatively – the Count recalled his wife's astonishment at the length of DeRossi's proboscis – and moved his head to and fro. The Count perceived that DeRossi had not, in fact, given much thought to the event. That meant he expected it to be the kind of trial colonial courts routinely gave African defendants.

"I see it as something that could have a deep influence on the colony," began the Count. "Not at all routine."

DeRossi nodded, waiting for the Count to reveal the direction he wanted their talk – and the trial - to take.

"I see it as an opportunity for the administration to educate both the settlers and the Congolese about judicial proceedings."

"Yes, I agree," said DeRossi, now able to align himself on the same side as the Governor-General. "What exactly do you have in mind?"

"Primarily," explained the Count, "it must be fair."

"Of course," agreed DeRossi. "I think we have discussed this." He rubbed his nose again, stared at the ceiling, and inquired. "Remind me of exactly what you mean."

"I mean that the outcome should actually be the result that evolves from the trial itself. There should be nothing to suggest that the outcome was pre-arranged."

"Hmm," observed DeRossi. "I must say it seems pretty obvious that sedition was involved. That's what the settlers think."

The infernal weakling, thought the Count. He has already decided the case. "Let the evidence show that," he suggested mildly.

"Of course," agreed the judge. "I'm sure it will."

"I see your courtroom as a kind of classroom," said the Count.

"Mmm," murmured DeRossi. "In what way exactly?"

"It needs to demonstrate that justice is fair. It's impartial." The Count had arrived at a difficult point. He studied DeRossi for a moment, wondering how persuadable he might be, then plunged ahead. "By impartial I mean that Kimbangu must be seen as being judged in the same way that a settler would be. Or a government officer."

DeRossi looked startled, no longer quite so agreeable. "Kimbangu's trial should be equivalent to a white man's trial?" He spoke as if considering such a concept pushed him beyond the boundaries of his permissable thought.

"Kimbangu is an unusual Congolese," noted the Count. "That much should be obvious to us all."

"Yes, but still he is a Congolese, a black man." DeRossi stared at the Governor-General, aghast, beginning to glimpse what the Count had in mind.

"But what's important, is it not," offered the Count, "is that he is a man? Like other men. Not that his skin is black."

"But, being black," said DeRossi, fumbling around, "he is not like other men. He is not like the settlers, for example."

The Count realized that he had pushed DeRossi beyond his point of comprehension. He must retreat to a position more digestible. "This notion of the courtroom as a classroom," he said. "Maybe it's important for Congolese – and settlers, too – to see that the same law applies equally to all of them. To all of us."

DeRossi frowned. The Count realized that he must speak more simply.

"I only present this as something to think about," Lippens gently assured him. For several moments the two men did not speak. The Count realized that he had played his hand. He rose to go. DeRossi stood. As they shook hands, the Count observed, "Let's not talk much about our having met."

DeRossi seemed to absorb that and nodded. "But let me ask," he said. "What would you consider an appropriate sentence?"

The Count realized that his visit had made less of an impression than he had hoped. "I wouldn't go there yet," he said. "He hasn't yet been proven guilty."

DeRossi could not refrain from asking, "Suppose he was adjudged guilty. . ."

The Count raised his hand to avoid this subject. "I would overstep my role if I offered suggestions." He smiled reassuringly. "But compassion always has a place in the classroom. And the courtroom. And the colony."

"But the settlers—" started DeRossi. Then he relented.

"Let's not worry about the settlers," suggested the Count. "This is a trial of an important Congolese. Let's just be sure that it teaches Congolese a little something about fairness and compassion, about how our justice system works."

At that the conference ended. When he and DeRossi said farewell, the Count could only hope that the judge would consider what he'd said. But as he walked back to his office, he doubted that was the case.

Over aperitifs as they talked before dinner, the Count told his wife, "Today I paid a visit to the largest nose in Boma."

She laughed. "Our friend Amadeo. How did it go?"

"We ought not to joke," said the Count. "Because, even if he keeps that nose to the grindstone—"

"You're a fine one to talk about not joking." She watched him devotedly, merriment in her eyes.

The truth was that the Countess's laughter helped the Count relax, gave him confidence, merited or not, that things would work out. He joined her in laughing and then became serious.

"In fact," he confided, "I'm not at all sure that he is up to the job that needs to be done."

"Did you try to coach him?"

"To the extent the situation permits."

"Don't be too conscientious about 'the situation.'"

"I tried to give him a few ideas.'

"Did he take them? Or shake them off?"

"He's very attuned to settler opinion. How settlers can believe that we foster a more peaceful, prosperous colony by killing off exceptional Congolese is quite beyond me."

"Maybe you should talk to them," suggested the Countess. "Admit that you have met with Kimbangu. Tell them that he has important contributions to offer the colony – if he's allowed to."

Hmm, thought the Count. That would take some courage. His wife's confidence in him was higher than his confidence in himself. "It is very hard to talk Count-to-commoner, Governor-General-to-settler. I'd need the Common Touch. I'm not sure I have it."

"I'm hardly the person to assure you that you do." The Countess laughed. She crossed the room to him, lifted the glass from his hand, and sat in his lap. She implored him, "Talk to me like a commoner, my love." They laughed together.

As the time of the prophet's trial approached, the Governor-General held several "listening sessions," as he called them, with settlers. He had Van Belle invite a dozen settlers for the ostensible purpose of his hearing their complaints, situations, ideas. He instructed Van Belle to have them talk about whatever was on their minds. Listening would be educational for the Count and perhaps reassuring to the settlers.

If he listened to them, he hoped perhaps they might be willing to listen to him. If the trial came up, perhaps he could suggest that evolved Congolese might be seen and employed as resources for the colony rather than a danger to it. He would not go so far as to point out that such an attitude could not be encouraged by executing Kimbangu. He hoped that the settlers might arrive at that conclusion on their own.

When he broached the "listening sessions" idea to his wife, reminding her that it was originally hers, she was enthusiastic and said he made her proud to be his partner. When he discussed the notion with Van Belle, the assistant wondered unhelpfully if they might not be more fruitful at a time when settler opinion was not so aroused; that meant after the Kimbangu trial had been held.

The sessions – there were three – were useful. They served to introduce the Governor-General to those he governed. It gave the settlers a chance to speak their minds and air their fears. The Count was struck by how much fear they expressed. They were adapting to a new environment: heat; relentless sun; vegetation, thick, tangled, and filled with possibly poisonous snakes, fruits, vines; noises. That adaptation had to be constant. They faced economic uncertainty. They felt high levels of discomfort about black people: their near nakedness, their drumming, their inclination to steal, the gibberish they spoke, their licentiousness and inclination to violence. The settlers stressed to Count Lippens their certainty that their safety lay in the administration's showing itself to be hard and swift.

When the Count tried deftly to suggest more enlightened notions, he felt waves of antagonism cross the room toward him. These waves assailed him at each of the three sessions. His efforts to move discussions to a point where he might suggest leniency toward Kimbangu seemed thwarted at every gathering.

"These settlers have difficult lives," he told the Countess after his exposure to them. "They came to Africa, hoping to better their prospects. They're contending with elements they didn't expect to confront. It's hard for them not to be wary of what they see as savages."

"Were you able to talk back and forth with them?" she asked.

The Count smiled ruefully. "I think I, too, am contending with elements I did not expect to confront."

"Poor Maurice!" she smiled supportively. "Then you weren't able to talk about Kimbangu's plight."

"Only very tangentially. I said I had met some educated Congolese, mainly mission-educated. I hoped we could make allies of them. It did not serve any purpose to regard them as enemies."

"Did that get across?"

"Maybe. I'm not optimistic." He stood, ready to call an end to his day. "I still think the best possibility is to get Kimbangu out of Bas-Congo until all this excitement dies down. By then the settlers will either have made a go of it or gone home. But it is clear now that we are headed for a trial."

As the couple walked to their bedroom, the Count realized that he had not shared some news with his wife. "Here's something that will interest you," he told her. "I received a note marked personal on the envelope today." The Countess perked up. This was unusual. "From our friend Morel, the young man with the famous mustache."

"And how is he?"

"Flourishing, I take it."

The Countess laughed. "He's found a friend."

"He took your advice and went to an enlightened convent school. Her name is Titi. She's settling in. He's not sure of her age, maybe sixteen, old enough out here to begin a life work of pleasing a man. He seems quite content and sent you his best regards."

The Countess said, "It's nice to have some happy news."

NINETEEN

A T DINNER THE EVENING BEFORE THE PROCEEDING against Kimbangu was to begin Countess Joanna asked her husband, "Will you be attending this trial?"

"You know I can't," he said.

"You look a little shamefaced saying that," she observed.

"It's DeRossi's show. I can't be seen to interfere." He looked at her, apology in his eyes, a knife held in one hand, a fork in the other. "Please understand. This is not cowardice."

The Countess laughed. "I wouldn't blame you if it were."

"I am very concerned," he admitted, laying down his utensils. "Kimbangu has no representation. DeRossi's weak. He lacks confidence. If I appear at the trial, he will shoot regular glances at me for tips about proceeding."

"Tips?"

"Signals. The courtroom will be full of settlers. If I am there, they will be watching me. If I scratch my nose or rub my chin or pull at my ear--" The Countess mimicked him, scratching her nose, rubbing her chin. "You have it precisely right, my dear," the Count praised her. "If I'm in the courtroom and do any pulling at my ear, settlers will scream that I am sending DeRossi signals."

The Countess pulled provocatively at her ear.

The Count smiled, amused. "Who would interpret that as a signal?"

"A *demimondaine*, I suppose," said the Countess. "I don't happen to know any."

"Nor do I, I hasten to add." They laughed together. The Count grew serious and regarded her imploringly. "As a matter of fact," he said, "I was hoping you would go."

The Countess was taken by surprise. "Me go? Without you?"

"I need eyes and ears there." He paused and added, "Especially if you are unobtrusive."

Finally the Countess asked, "How can I go? It's not really a trial. The outcome is already known. And a day spent watching that long-nosed judge? I couldn't." She cocked her head flirtatiously. "Can't you send Van Belle?"

"He can't be there for the same reason I can't."

"He might pull at his ear."

"Precisely."

"So I need to be a good wifey." He gazed at her beseechingly. "Especially if I am unobtrusive." He nodded. "Your dinner's getting cold."

They finished their meal in silence, the Countess contemplating what she must do. Finally she observed, "In this place it is not actually possible for the Governor-General's wife to appear unobtrusively anywhere."

"I do know that." He added, "And a beautiful woman always--"

"Oh, posh. Not that." She suggested, "Let's both do the trial and make *causes célèbres* of ourselves."

"That's exactly what we must not do."

"Please come with me."

The Governor-General shook his head. "But you'll go." The Countess raised her eyebrows with forbearance. "For the settlers, be above reproach. Say little. Take notes."

"And do not pull at your ear."

The trial of Simon Kimbangu convened in the largest building in Boma. It had a corrugated metal roof, an earthen floor and walls only four feet tall, the space between them and the roof open to the air. This feature defeated the stuffiness of a closed space and permitted air to flow through the structure. Also rain. If a storm occurred, rain blew in. The sound of the rain on the metal roof, particularly if it was a downpour, made it difficult to hear. If the rain was light, the sound of raindrops falling on the roof was sometimes welcome, pleasantly distracting. There were three rows of chairs, for whites only. Behind them stood benches. These had no backrests; that made long-term sitting unpleasant. In any case, Congolese were discouraged from attending trials.

At one side of the hall a dais had been erected. Judge DeRossi presided from this dais. Prosecutors sat below him to his left and right. For the safety of the proceeding Kimbangu, alone, without legal representation, sat housed in a closed space with a swinging door and two guards.

Countess Lippens dressed for the trial as unobtrusively as possible. She wore her simplest dress and a sun hat that she removed inside the courtroom. When she entered the building, people opened the way for her; an official escorted her to the first row of chairs and seated her on the center aisle. To her annoyance, which she covered, the official insisted on introducing her to the members of the prosecution.

To her embarrassment everyone in the room knew that she was there. She felt conspicuous and unusually self-conscious, but she did not sense any hostility. That changed as soon as she removed a small notebook from her large purse. In it she would record her observations.

At that moment, knowing settlers were watching her, wondering what she would write, she felt a negative curiosity directed toward her. She wondered if the negativity was real and hostile or merely the workings of her imagination.

At this moment Monsignor Van Rolse arrived and made his way up the center aisle. Seeing her, he offered his hand and they shook. The churchman took the seat beside her. When he saw her notebook, he whispered, making a little joke. "Countess, will you be covering the trial for *La Libre Belgique?*"

"I hadn't thought of that," she replied. "What a good idea!"

After this exchange she imagined that Van Rolse would notice every time she wrote in the book. Her self-consciousness increased. She glanced around the hall and saw other churchmen positioned about the room.

When the defendant was brought in, accompanied by guards, a wave of hostility swept across the hall. The Countess felt it physically. The guards brought the manacled Kimbangu forward. The Countess saw settlers watching him with expressions of such rage that she turned away from them. Her sympathies went out to the prophet. Like everyone else, she watched him. But unlike everyone else, when Kimbangu looked at her, she gave him a small smile and nodded her head. Despite this gesture of reassurance, Kimbangu seemed uncertain and confused about what was happening to him.

The Monsignor whispered to her again. "Did you—"

She did not let him finish. "The hostility in here is overwhelming," she said. "Don't you feel it crushing us?"

"It's hatred of the anti-Christ," the Monsignor explained.

The Countess managed to get through the day. When she could not bear the trial or it bored her, she gazed at the Africans keeping track of the proceeding standing outside the courtroom walls, looking in.

That evening at dinner the Countess avoided the subject of the trial. Afterwards she led her husband to the small parlor where she would brief him. After they settled themselves, each with a cup of coffee, she began by saying, "It is quite an unpleasant job you've given me."

"You're good to do it." He lightly teased her. "Were you unobstrusive?"

"Hardly. Monsignor Van Rolse did me the honor of sitting beside me. Repellent man! He may not be the type to peek down a woman's *décolletage*, but I could hardly make a note without him peering at that."

"It's because you are so beautiful, my love," the Count said with a laugh.

"You're relighting fires in him long dead—"

"Oh, please. Don't start that!" She stuck her tongue out at him.

He smiled and took a swallow of coffee. "How is the trial?"

"A barbaric ritual, a kind of bear-baiting. As usual the bear can't defend himself."

"Is it really so awful?" The Count assumed his wife was having a good time exaggerating. She gazed at him, annoyed. "Tell me," he urged, his tone no longer playful. "Is it awful?"

"Yes. Poor Kimbangu! The settlers' hostility to him surrounds us like a fog." The Countess drank some coffee to let her husband absorb that. Then she added, quite matter-of-factly, "The worst part is knowing how it's going to end. They're going to kill him. They know it. He knows it. Sitting in that courtroom is practically an act of courage."

The Count said quietly, "They are not going to kill him."

"You wouldn't say that if you were there." She added, "DeRossi is an embarrassment." She poured them both more coffee.

"You know I've tried to groom him for the job. If I could exile him to 'the farthest reaches of the colony,' I'd do that."

The Countess smiled. "The best moments of the day were when five or six butterflies flew into the courtroom. For a moment everyone watched them. Humanity returned to that vile place. One of the butterflies landed on my shoulder—"

"One angel recognizes another."

"—And then flew off." She grew pensive for a moment, thinking of the butterfly. "I wanted to say, 'Not me! Not me! Land on him!'"

"Did you take notes?" the Count asked.

"I was as modest as a mouse," she assured him. "Or hoped I was with the Monsignor glaring at me whenever I wrote."

"What a good girl you are!" said the Count, teasing again.

The Countess took her notebook from the large purse and sorted through it.

The Count now became totally focused on his wife's report. "How is Kimbangu bearing up?" he asked.

"Pretty well," the Countess admitted admiringly. "Considering that he's there alone, without an ally in the hall. The man might as well be naked."

"What was said?" The Count took a pad and began to make notes himself.

"DeRossi charged Kimbangu with organizing a plot against the colonial government."

"He knows there is no evidence of that," the Count grumbled. Now that they had gotten down to business, he tried to mask before his wife how defensive he felt about the trial, about court officials brazenly misapplying the law. And this while he served as Governor-General. Before his wife, it was unnecessary to feel embarrassment. But he did. "How did Kimbangu respond to the charges?" he asked.

"Denied them. DeRossi accused him of inciting people to abandon their jobs and not pay taxes. He denied that as well." After a moment she asked, "Could he have done that"

The Count sipped his coffee. Finally he said, "Given all the trembling and shouting, he might have." Maybe it was well to suggest that the state did have something of a case. "Undoubtedly the *n'gunza* did."

The Countess consulted her notes. "There were questions about Nkamba. Kimbangu claimed that people went there on their own. To hear God's message and seek salvation."

The Governor-General nodded and made a note.

The Countess searched through what she had written. "Something about taxes. I can't remember what." She looked up from her notes and asked, "Why all this concern for taxes? Tax receipts from Africans can't amount to five papayas. And the church is also after them to give money to the priests."

The Count explained, "Belgium can't run a colony that's supposed to pay for itself when workers don't pay taxes—"

The Countess finished his words for him. "And run off, certain that the end of the world is at hand?" Then she asked, "Is that how the world ends? We still owe taxes?"

The Count bestowed an indulgent smile on his wife. She continued, "The Fathers indoctrinate them in Christian mythology and then panic if they believe it." She threw up her arms. "Yes, yes, I know. We must be seen as supporting the Fathers."

"Did DeRossi ask Kimbangu if he were a prophet?"

"He claimed to be an envoy." The Countess looked at the direct quotation she had written in her notebook. "'By the divine power the Lord Jesus Christ gave me,' he said. 'I am not a prophet, but a special envoy of the Lord Jesus Christ.'"

"Did that upset our friend the Monsignor?"

"I heard a low grumbling in his throat." She added, "You can bet he and his minions are discussing those words right now over their whiskeys."

"The minions are in the courtroom?"

"Hanging from the ceiling."

The Count nodded. He expected as much.

The Countess continued to scan her notes. "DeRossi asked Kimbangu about Kinshasa." She found what she had written of the exchange. "'Were you in contact with the Marxist black American group, the Garveyites? What do you say?' And Kimbangu replied, 'That is totally false.'"

The Count stood to move about the room, too distressed to remain seated.

"DeRossi claimed that Kimbangu had his followers collect money," reported the Countess. "He charged, 'Wasn't that because you were preparing people to buy arms to fight against us?'"

"So we broadcast our fears to the world."

"Kimbangu insisted he did not ask people to pay him" – she quoted his words – "'for their salvation.'" She watched her husband wend his way around the furniture. "That's rather sweet, don't you think?" She gave a maternal smile. "He said money was given voluntarily to feed the people who came to Nkamba. He condemned violence. Christ taught against violence, he said."

The Countess put down her notes and gazed at her husband, wondering where they would be in two years, in five years. "You know I want us to leave the Congo with your reputation burnished."

"This Kimbangu business is very bad luck for us," he replied.

Still watching the worried man moving about the room, she asked, "When the Monsignor and the planters and the business people all said, 'Crush this man—'"

With a fury the Count cried, "'Crush the bug! Crush the bug!' They said it. They still say it." He resumed pacing about.

"Don't they know the world is watching?"

The Count said nothing. He doubted that the world had any notion of what was happening in Boma. Or would care if it did know.

The Countess returned to a matter that deeply bothered her. "Why is Kimbangu not permitted a defense counsel?" she asked once again.

"I've told you about that," the Count said tiredly. "DeRossi claims he could not find a local lawyer who would do it. And I could not induce any man in the metropole to take it up." He asked, "Why would a man want to come all the way out here from Europe just to lose a case?"

"How hard did DeRossi look?"

The Count shrugged and paced for several moments before answering. "The whites are terrified that the blacks will get the upper hand," he said. "That unless we come down hard, we will *give* them the upper hand. So let's get it over with quickly. The settlers and the palace want this over *now.*" He emphasized the word "*now.*" After a moment he added, "We are a tiny country with a shopkeeper mentality."

The Countess watched her husband as he paced. "We have no business running a colony forty times our size. Where the settlers are frightened all the time." She ordered her notes and returned them to her purse. "I hope you will forgive me if I cannot take another day of this."

The Count nodded, deep in thought, but having heard her. "We are moral midgets," he said. "I wonder what the Belgian Congo would be if the Katanga's mineral wealth did not make us all so rich."

Several days passed. The trial of Simon Kimbangu gripped Boma, but neither the Count nor his wife attended the proceeding. By rigorous self-discipline they managed to banish it from their thoughts.

After dinner in the small parlor the Countess read her husband a letter they had received from their nephew in Belgium, her brother Hugo's son. It contained photographs of the nephew and a young woman, his "very good friend." The Count gazed intently at the photos as his wife finished reading the letter aloud, then almost immediately reread it. When she finished, the Count asked, "Does he intend to marry—"

"Don't ask that, please," implored the Countess. "He's only twenty, too young to marry."

"We didn't marry till I was in my thirties."

"He can't be thinking of marrying someone we've never met," she said. Then, thinking out loud, she added, "I don't suppose we can return home for a wedding just yet, can we?"

The Count did not reply. He was considering a letter of counsel to the nephew. What could he advise? If the girl came from a good family, as what little information they possessed seemed to indicate, he could not suggest, could he, that the young man "enjoy her" while their passions for each other were at flood crest? Such advice was too worldly for a father. Would it be acceptable from an uncle? Probably not. The Lippenses did not even know if the passions had reached "flood crest." But if not, why the photos?

As the Count contemplated what to write, a knock came at the door. He shot a look at his wife, baffled. Who could be knocking? It was past nine o'clock. The servants had retired.

The door opened. Van Belle entered. "Please forgive us," said the assistant. "Us?" wondered the Count. Who was "us"? "I know that it's quite late, but the circumstances are—"

Into the room walked Judge DeRossi.

Surprised, the Count rose to his feet and retreated across the room. The Countess held the nephew's letter and photograph against her chest as if they would shield her. The Count was not only surprised by the judge's presence in his residence, he was appalled.

He saw immediately that the visit might represent an opportunity to affect the outcome of the trial. But he had given up all thought of influencing that outcome. Still the men's arrival could mean only one thing. "What are you doing here?" the Count demanded.

"Excellency," began the judge. "Please excuse me." Exhaustion wrapped DeRossi like a cloak.

"I mean no offense," insisted the Count, "but you are not welcome here." He must appear to disapprove of the visit, even to the point of being discourteous.

The Countess's training asserted itself. She rose and started toward the visitors. "Please!" she cried. "Excuse my husband." She approached the men and offered her hand. "Of course, you are welcome."

"No, he's not!" exclaimed the Count. "I'm sorry, *messieurs*. Forgive me." He took his wife by the elbow and drew her away. "But a visit at this hour. It can only be about the trial. And that is not the business of the Governor-General! I have nothing to do with it!"

The visitors looked abashed, like schoolboys scolded by a headmaster.

The Countess glanced at her husband. Why was he being so abrupt? He rarely acted this way. Then it occurred to her that this was a guise.

The Count turned to Van Belle. "Who knows you're here?"

"No one," said the assistant, distressed that he had succumbed to DeRossi's insistence that he consult the Governor-General. "We came in my car. We entered at the servants' door."

These words calmed the Count. He glanced at Van Belle, who was genuinely abashed to have called so late. He inspected DeRossi. The man was a bundle of nerves, even smaller in stature than usual. The flesh of his face was pasty. Dark circles surrounded eyes sunken beneath heavy eyebrows. The nose had grown even longer.

"What shall I do?" he asked the Count. He was hardly able to utter the words.

The Count said, mildly now, "Do your duty."

"But to whom?" implored DeRossi. "This man Kimbangu? Or the colony?" He lifted his eyes to the Count as if he were a beggar pleading for alms.

"I have a duty to the colony, don't I? If I don't execute him, don't I place the colony in jeopardy?"

"I'll take care of the colony," the Count stated, refusing to give alms. "You do right by the law. You have a duty to it, too, you know."

"But what does that mean?" DeRossi stumbled to a chair. He sat, his hands clasped between his knees, eyes staring at the floor.

The Count stepped toward him. "For God's sake, man! You know the law. Has he broken it? Don't come whimpering to me!"

The Countess moved beside her husband and put a hand on his forearm. He regarded her, knowing she was counseling patience, sympathy, even fellow-feeling. He paused for a moment, collecting himself. He leaned toward DeRossi and said almost compassionately, "We are running a vast colony here. Your job is justice. Mine is administration. There must be no question but that you reached your verdict independent of the administration." In a compassionate way he made it very clear, "I will not have it said that the Governor-General told you how to rule."

DeRossi looked up at him beseechingly. "I don't know what to do."

The Count turned to Van Belle, his eyes inquiring, "What do I do?" The aide spread his hands, mystified.

"What is my duty?" sniveled DeRossi.

Finally, more gently, the Count said, "Render the judgment you consider fair."

"But fair to whom?"

"The person on trial," said the Count, as if he were the judge's older brother. "The defendant, of course."

DeRossi weighed this counsel. Finally he asked, "Is that what the palace wants?"

"The trial is here," said the Count quietly. "Not in Brussels."

"But what does the palace want?" asked DeRossi.

The Count nodded to Van Belle and led him from the parlor. As they left the room, the Count muttered, "If I had nails and a hammer, I would go to the office and make that fetish yelp!"

As the door closed, DeRossi remained seated, his eyes seeing nothing as they stared at the floor. The Countess observed the judge. She moved toward him without speaking. She wanted to comfort him as she might one of the children she had left in Belgium or the nephew who might marry prematurely. But she sensed that she must say nothing. DeRossi looked up at her. "Countess, I want to do what's right." The judge spoke so softly, with such lack of confidence, that she could hardly hear him. "But it is very difficult."

In the hall the Count asked Van Belle. "What's going on here? Does DeRossi have contacts in the palace that worry him?" He added, "And should worry us?"

"Not that I've heard of."

"Then the palace is not the problem."

"If the palace desired a certain verdict," Van Belle said simply, "we would know. And he would know."

"Does he want to shift the blame for whatever happens on us?"

Van Belle shrugged. That meant, "Of course. Why not?"

The Count considered this opinion. "Is he truly afraid the colony will burst into rebellion unless he executes this man?"

"His neighbors believe that. So he believes it."

The Count mulled this problem. "The palace can't want an execution," he said, thinking aloud.

With scorn Van Belle remarked, "He's afraid. If he doesn't execute Kimbangu, he thinks his neighbors will throw him to the crocodiles."

The Count nodded, agreeing. "He wants to immunize himself from criticism by letting it be whispered, 'The Governor-General gave him instructions.'"

Van Belle shrugged.

The Count and his assistant returned to the small parlor. The Count looked around for a chair and drew it up to DeRossi. He sat in it and leaned toward the judge, suddenly an exemplar of patience. "In the Free State days," the Count began, "Africans were killed gratuitously. Without regard to their rights or their humanity. That time has ended." DeRossi stared at the floor, like a schoolboy being lectured. More patiently the Count added, "We have talked about how your courtroom can become a kind of classroom for the colony."

DeRossi nodded, still looking at the floor.

"And we've talked about fairness and compassion. We talked about how this trial can be seen as judging a black man as fairly as a trial would judge a white man."

DeRossi said nothing.

"Simon Kimbangu is a prophet, a healer," continued the Count. "He has inspired excitement among Congolese. But there is not a shred of evidence that he's committed a crime. Have you heard such evidence?" When DeRossi did not answer, the Count persisted. "Do you really think Kimbangu planned to overthrow the state? Do you think he collected money to buy arms? Does the prosecution show evidence of this?"

DeRossi very narrowly shook his head.

"Evidence shows that he was healing people in Nkamba," said the Count. "Feeding them. Forbidding lewd dancing, polygamy. Law requires you to judge according to the evidence. That's what you can do in the courtroom that is a classroom."

DeRossi glanced up at the Count with a look of terror in his eyes.

"That may seem to require as much courage as you've ever shown," said the Count. "But I'm sure you can do it. I have confidence in you." The Count reached out to give DeRossi a supportive pat. He rested his hand on the man's shoulder.

"Doing the right thing strengthens a man. It emboldens his courage."

"But what is the right thing?" asked DeRossi. "Let the law be the law.

"Let the law speak, not Amadeo DeRossi."

DeRossi seemed to shrink from this task.

"You can do it," encouraged the Count. "We both know that if the trial is fair, the charges against Kimbangu cannot be sustained." The Count looked deeply into DeRossi's eyes. "Do you acknowledge that?"

Finally the judge nodded.

"So it would be a grave miscarriage of justice to execute this man."

DeRossi could not bring himself to agree.

"Wouldn't it?" persisted the Count. He squeezed DeRossi's shoulder. Finally the judge nodded his agreement.

"We are trying to establish a new era here," said the Count. "You have the opportunity to help us take a great step forward. Grab that opportunity!"

DeRossi's eyes showed a flicker of courage. He sat up.

"We are building civilization here," emphasized the Count. "Our purpose here cannot be simply to strip this place of its resources. We cannot build civilization if we execute every Congolese who shows enterprise, talent – especially not one with the capacity to heal."

DeRossi smiled at the Count's enthusiasm.

"Twenty years from now," the Count went on, "when progress has been made, you'll be able to say with pride, 'I helped make that progress a reality. I judged a man not by prejudices and paranoia, but by the law. I refused to execute an innocent man.'"

What DeRossi was thinking was written on his face.

"When you come to announcing the verdict," the Count advised, understanding the judge's predicament, "fill the courtroom with soldiers of the Force Publique. Announce that the troops are there to maintain order. After the verdict, have the defendant led away, completely surrounded by Force

Publique guards. And have them stay with him – I will help you on this – until Kimbangu has departed Boma."

DeRossi nodded. "But what will we do with Kimbangu?"

The Count lifted his hand from DeRossi's shoulder and rose from the chair. "We rusticate him. Until all this furor has ended."

"Is that fair?" asked the judge.

"I acknowledge that it's not," said the Count. "The Court has an obligation to protect the colony." He leaned toward the judge, "And the defendant. We don't want to acquit the defendant, then release him into a killing field. There's a town upriver where he might be safe from people who are so afraid of him that they would kill him." The Count added, "Think how proud you'll be – and your family will be – of the step forward you helped this colony make."

DeRossi stood. He asked exactly how Kimbangu's extrication would be handled if he were sentenced only to rustication. The Count said, "Perhaps it is best if you do not know. I say that to protect you."

DeRossi considered for a moment, then nodded his agreement. At last with great relief he said, "I'm glad we talked, Governor-General. I think what you have told me provides the answer. I will try to let the law strengthen me." He and the Count shook hands.

The Count requested, "Be sure that no one sees you leaving. And tell no one of this meeting. If any suggestion of it slips out, my office will deny it ever happened."

The two men left. The Count sat exhaustedly in a chair well away from the one DeRossi occupied. His wife watched him, feeling proud, but careful not to intrude upon his thoughts. He sat, holding his head, reminding himself that he was being the best Governor-General he could be. Sometimes that required tolerating secret, nocturnal meetings. This one had been inappropriate, but on the whole, quite useful. He had argued forcefully for the best arrangement that could be made for the prophet. DeRossi had listened and, he hoped, had been convinced. He uncovered his face, turned to his wife, and asked, "Well?"

"You can be eloquent when you choose," she observed.

He laughed tiredly. "With luck," he said, "we have saved Simon Kimbangu's life."

The Countess came to him and rewarded him a kiss.

TWENTY

O N THE DAY FOLLOWING THE VISIT OF DEROSSI and Van Belle, the Count felt in good spirits. He had made clear that he considered their appearance inappropriate; he hoped the fact of the visit would remain unknown. Even so, he regarded it as a success. Despite its unseemliness, he had been able to impress upon DeRossi the lack of any real evidence against Kimbangu and therefore of his innocence. He had been able to suggest to the judge measures he could take to protect himself while seeming to protect the defendant. He regarded his explanation of a vision of the colony's future – that it was trying to build an enlightened civilization in Africa – to have been rather well-expressed.

True, Brussels had signaled its interest in the trial. That meant he had overstepped the boundaries he should maintain regarding it. But as Belgium's top official in the colony perhaps that was his duty – and his right. There was no point in being punctilious. Rather it was crucial that the trial reach an appropriate outcome, one that protected an innocent man while taking into account the colony's interests and the settlers' fears, whether or not they were justified. The Count hoped that DeRossi would sentence Kimbangu along the lines he had suggested. Realistically, he estimated the chances of that happening at fifty-fifty.

Judge DeRossi gave notice that he would announce his verdict and pass sentence on the same occasion. The Count made arrangements for Kimbangu to be taken immediately from the courtroom to the Force Publique encampment outside Boma and held there until the Governor-General issued new orders. The Count ordered the barge, usually reserved for the Governor-General's use, to be made ready to take the Count and Countess on a week-long sight-seeing trip up river, a deserved vacation after the tensions of the trial. If DeRossi pronounced a rustication sentence, Kimbangu would be secretly transferred to the barge and taken upriver. Van Belle had arranged for officers in Coquilhatville to stand ready to requisition a house outside the town where Kimbangu could live out his rustication.

As the Count made ready for a possible "rustication verdict," Van Belle advised him to act to control reactions against such a verdict. He feared that many would regard rustication as too lenient. He suggested that the Count invite Boma notables to join him in the Governor-General's office when the verdict was announced. Monsignor Van Rolse of the Catholic Church and Hans Bogaerts representing planters accepted the invitation. So did territorial administrator Léon-Georges Morel who traveled to Boma to attend. General LeMoine of the Force Publique pleaded the possibility of public disorder; he chose to stay near the courtroom. Settler leaders, known to the Count from the "listening groups." convinced themselves that the Governor-General was too liberal. They suspected that his intention was to compromise them. They declined his invitation. They would maintain pressure on DeRossi by forcing him to appear before them in the courtroom.

The Count and his wife surveyed the chairs that had been arranged in his office. She whispered to him, "Did you notice! Morel shaved off his mustache. What in the world happened?"

"Titi acted," her husband suggested. "Titi?" He repeated the name as if tasting it. "Dark as chocolate. But sweeter. I suppose she insisted. When he kissed her nakedness, she could not stop giggling."

"And," the Countess whispered, "he could not function while she giggled."

The Count spoke sternly into his wife's ear. "No laughing during sex!" They chuckled together.

The Count went back to surveying chairs. "This is a smaller turnout than I had hoped for," he remarked.

"What does it mean?" the Countess asked.

"I'm not sure," he confessed. "Ordinarily these men would not turn down an invitation from the Governor-General."

"Is that a warning of some kind to us?"

"Perhaps. Maybe they're embarrassed, knowing the evidence against Kimbangu doesn't support the kind of verdict they want."

The Countess knew that her husband was so hopeful that DeRossi would deliver a rustication verdict as to arrange for the prophet's quick and secret removal from Boma. She hoped that DeRossi would not disappoint. She left her husband to attend to the coffee and pastry she had arranged to be brought from the residence.

When the guests assembled, the atmosphere was tense, electric with anticipation. With the help of retainers from the residence, the Countess made sure all guests had refreshment. Once they were served, the Count nodded to Van Belle. He excused himself and went to the pavilion serving as the courtroom to receive the sentence once it was announced.

The talk among the guests ceased. Neither the Count nor his wife attempted to revive it. The Countess sat, saucer and coffee cup balanced on her knee, hoping that her presence might lighten the atmosphere. The men ignored her. None of them sat. Several paced. Finally the Countess heard young Morel say, "There can be problems, I suppose, whichever way the verdict goes." No one else spoke. Out of nervousness Morel persisted, "If we hang him, God forbid—"

"Why 'God forbid'?" challenged the Monsignor. "God expects us to exterminate heresies."

The Countess quietly, in horror, stared at her coffee cup. She could imagine her husband biting his tongue.

"Won't hanging set the stage for a rebellion?" asked Morel, timidly challenging the churchman. "We will have brought it on ourselves."

The Count wanted to clap Morel on the back, but did not move from the desk where he sat.

Van Rolse examined Morel as if he were an insect and turned away.

"I'm hoping for a surprise," Morel continued. "Rustication ought to do the job. Rusticating the *n'gunza* has calmed things down in Bas-Congo."

"If the sentence is too lenient," prophesied Bogaerts, "we will see whites chase poor DeRossi right into the great river." He laughed heartily. "Poor DeRossi will be swept out to sea."

"Let the sentence be death," asserted the Monsignor. "Let us cut off the head of the serpent."

"Excuse my asking," Morel began tentatively.

The Countess thought nervousness made Morel keep talking. She wondered what the true story was about the shaving of his mustache. Had that occurred in a private ceremony for Titi alone or was it performed before his entire community? Morel did not finish his question.

"I hope DeRossi stops short of a death penalty," Bogaerts declared.

That assertion pleased the Count. "Are you serious?" asked the Monsignor.

"If Kimbangu's executed," explained the planter, "very soon rumors will fly that he has resurrected himself. That he's been seen in this place and that. Shrines will be set up."

Morel laughed. "Every fellow resembling Kimbangu will claim—"

"My young friend," interrupted the Monsignor, "that would keep you very busy." Then he warned, "We must prevent that happening. I say, Chop the body into pieces. Let his followers see us do it. Then just let them try to claim a resurrection."

The Countess gave a cry. "You can't be serious!"

"Entirely," the churchman assured her. "Nail prints and a spear wound in the side: followers could work with that. Putting together severed legs, severed arms? Our friend Kimbangu won't be resurrecting that."

Van Belle entered. A hush fell over the assembled. He handed an envelope to the Count. The Count opened the envelope, withdrew the message, and read it. His wife examined him carefully for indications of his reaction. His mouth tightened at the corners. She felt concern.

"A severe penalty," the Count announced, trying to keep emotion from his voice.

The Monsignor smiled. "Thank God!"

Bogaerts shrugged his shoulders.

"You might take seats," the Count suggested. "No need to pace any longer."

While the guests seated themselves, the Count read through the document a second time. He gazed at the others: the Monsignor and the planter with Countess Lippens; Morel by himself; Van Belle standing beside the Governor-General.

Almost at random the Count picked out sentences to read. "This document states," said the Count; then he read: "'Kimbangu was recognized by the doctors as sound of body and spirit and is by consequence responsible for all his acts.'" The Count surveyed the guests, then returned his gaze to the sentencing document. He read: "'His fits of nerves are nothing but shamming.'" The Count glanced at his wife. She sensed how deeply these words angered him, but he masked his reaction.

Again he scanned the document and read, "'The goal pursued was that of destroying the authority of the state.'" His eyes skimmed the sentences. He read: "'It remains established that by his acts, remarks, schemes, writings, songs, and his history dictated by himself' – quite a list – 'Simon Kimbangu has set himself up as a savior of the black race in indicating the white as the enemy.'"

The Count read through the remainder of the sentencing text in silence. Then he read aloud: "'The sect of prophets must be considered organized in order to bear attacks on the security of the state, a sect hidden under the veil of a new religion.'" He went on: "'The march of events could have led fatally to revolt.'"

"And?" asked the Monsignor.

The Count read from the sentencing text: "'The prisoner will be transported to the penal colony at Elisabethville, Katanga. There he will receive one hundred twenty lashes—'"

"*Mon Dieu*" exclaimed Bogaerts.

"'And be executed,'" concluded the Count.

"That takes care of Monsieur Kimbangu," declared the Monsignor, his face beaming. "We have crushed the bug."

"And shown the world," observed the Governor-General, "that in the Belgian Congo the slightest whisper of African yearning is answered with cruelty."

The Countess gazed at her husband, knowing how deeply he wished that DeRossi had followed his guidance.

"The court did what had to be done," said the Monsignor.

"But my god!" said Bogaerts. "One hundred twenty lashes from a rhino hide whip. I tell you: there will not be much left to execute."

The Count turned to Morel. "Go immediately to Nkamba," he instructed. "Take a detachment of troops with you. An adequate detachment this time. Maintain public order down there."

"Yes, Governor," replied Morel. He immediately left the room.

The Count looked about the office. "That seems to conclude our business for this morning," he said and stood behind his desk. "Thank you for coming." Van Rolse and Bogaerts got to their feet. They shook hands all around and departed. The Countess rose and looked tenderly at her husband.

"I know you are disappointed, Maurice. But it is done now. It can't hurt us."

"I ordered the barge prepared for us," he said. "Shall we take an overnight trip on the river? Maybe as far as Matadi and back?"

"Yes, I'd like that. I'll pack a valise." The Countess smiled with relief. At last for both of them there would be an escape from the tensions of Boma.

After the Countess departed, the Count asked, "Did you expect this, Van Belle?"

"I did, sir." The Count nodded, disappointed. "If you drank in saloons where the settlers gather, you would know that DeRossi was under unendurable pressure to come down hard."

The Count felt a deep sense of both humiliation and betrayal. He moved away from Van Belle, went to the window, and gazed out across the river to the opposite bank, his posture slumped, defeated. Finally he turned back to Van Belle. He said, "I am not sure that colonialism is an enterprise worthy of honorable men."

"As with all things we take the bad with the good."

The Count gazed at Africa: so difficult for white men to absorb, understand, and give themselves to it. He said, "I will write a memorandum urging the King to commute the sentence."

Van Belle did not reply. He asked, "Shall I prepare a dispatch with this news?"

The Count continued to survey Africa. Finally he said, "Yes, of course." Then he asked, "How soon will Kimbangu be transferred to Katanga?"

"It will be several weeks. The palace must sign off before the state executes him."

The Count stood erect as if ready to take command again. He told Van Belle, "I would like to meet with Kimbangu before he's sent to Katanga. Can you arrange that?"

"Yes, sir."

"As before. Top secret." Van Belle nodded. The Count had the impression that his aide was not enthusiastic about the meeting. Perhaps, after all, he was not disappointed with the sentence of execution.

"I'll arrange it," said Van Belle. He withdrew.

Once he was alone, the Count glanced about the office. Yes, he would be glad to escape from it for a day or two. He observed the African fetish, nails imbedded into its chest. It was implacable in its expression and fearful in the enormity of its genital assertion. This, he felt, was what the settlers feared, what they could not take a chance on forgiving. He regarded it only as a sculpture.

The Count felt someone behind him. He turned to see Leopold II staring down at him. With disapproval. The Count turned his back on him. He walked in circles about the office. He felt that both the king and the fetish disapproved of him, the king for weakness, the sculpture for his inability to have his instructions translated into action. He determined to disregard them both. Standing fully erect, he gazed at the portrait and spoke aloud to the old man, "Five years would have been sufficient."

TWENTY-ONE

OUT ON THE WATER, AS THE BARGE PLOWED upstream against the current, Count and Countess Lippens promised themselves that they would have a day to themselves, one in which they did not think of the Belgian Congo. So long imprisoned in offices, they sat in the warm, comfortable sun, their faces protected from its rays by pith helmets. They rejoiced in the gentle flow of cool air wafting across their bodies. They reveled in the silence, interrupted only by the twitter of birds and by the songs about them lifted to the air by Congolese boatmen who hailed the barge from far off and sang about its splendors. They nibbled snacks that appeared out of nowhere and tempted their palates. They sniffed the aromas of wine and sipped it at their leisure. When they looked at the landscape, they did not see Africa. They saw what painters might, mere shapes and collections of colors.

When they hardly knew each other, the Count took the Countess boating on the Scheldt River in Flanders. They reminisced about that occasion and the Count confessed that it was then that he had decided to marry her. The Countess laughed doubtfully at this because the Count had a weakness for telling her the different occasions on which he had decided that they would marry. She assured him that she decided on the marriage earlier than he.

They talked about their children, who seemed to be well cared for and supervised by the Count's mother, learning Bible stories from her just as he had and, as a result, being grateful to escape back to their boarding schools. They talked about the nephew who had fallen in love at twenty and was thinking of marrying. The Count acknowledged that he had not yet written the letter of worldly counsel he had contemplated writing the young man. He considered that this was probably just as well since worldly counsel was rarely appreciated when the young were in the throes of first love.

The Countess asked her husband about his first loves and he denied having any before she swept him off his feet. When he asked her to tell about hers, she began to list them. He kissed her quite solidly and told her he was sure she had never known love until she knew it with him. She assured him that he was not the first man she had loved, though he was the best and certainly the most accomplished kisser.

They took a languid and leisurely nap together in the afternoon. When the barge neared Matadi, they stood on the deck and watched the town appear out of the landscape. They had stopped in the town briefly on their excursion to Reverend Parkins' mission station at Kimpese. This time they walked through the place, allowing settlers to wonder who the swells were without feeling any need to identify themselves. At dusk the barge chugged on a bit farther. During that time the Count and his lady enjoyed a simple dinner. The barge found an anchorage and spent the night at the river's edge. As the couple turned in, they thanked each other for a blissfully uncomplicated day.

The following morning the Count's duties reasserted themselves. He sat on the deck, mulling the memorandum of recommendations about Kimbangu he would write to the palace. Van Belle had prepared an official dispatch, reporting DeRossi's verdict and sentence. The Count had signed it before leaving on the excursion. It had been sent.

In his mulling the Count wondered how the verdict would be received in Brussels, possibly with disappointment, even horror, but more likely with relief. Factions of hardliners existed both at the palace and in the Ministry of Colonies. They would applaud DeRossi's verdict and the sentence. "Coming down hard" was their remedy for any African resistance, even for any flowering of Congolese initiative.

The Count knew the palace would receive letters from the Monsignor and settler groups, supporting execution and reinforcing the hardline views. He knew the palace would take careful readings of its subjects' desires. Their desires and the sentence they endorsed depressed the Count. He felt a sickness in his soul about the miscarriage of justice perpetrated on his watch.

The palace would expect a reaction from him. But what kind of reaction? "Courtiers are meant to give a king the advice he wants to hear." He had known this adage for many years. But he had no idea what the king himself thought. He could not imagine that the king supported an execution. But was he assigning the king his own views?

When formulating advice, a careful courtier would keep the hardliners' views in mind. But the Count had never considered himself a courtier, certainly not a flatterer. Nor did he regard himself as a creature of the Belgian colonial system; he would not act as if he were one. He spent the day on the river wondering how to articulate his conviction.

When he returned to the office, he paced between the fetish and the portrait trying to walk himself out of his dilemma. He slept badly. In periods of wakefulness he wandered about the residence, fearing that his Governor-Generalship would be stained by the Kimbangu business, by a show trial staged on his watch, especially by the prophet's execution.

But what to write the palace? His paralysis annoyed him. He thought of himself as having more character. He did not discuss the matter with his wife. He knew that she was aware of his nocturnal wanderings and understood their cause. He feared that her opinion of him was diminished.

Finally he found the courage to ask himself: What if the palace didn't like his recommendations? So what? Belgium was a postage stamp of a country. The king was a pip-squeak monarch. Enough of acting like a small-minded courtier! He would write what he felt. His confidence returned. He was who he was!

Once he came to this decision, the memo practically wrote itself. He explained that he had met with Kimbangu; he had interviewed the prophet himself. He was persuaded that Kimbangu was an authentic holy man, a healer; he had not conspired against the colony.

The trial, he wrote, had not been conducted according to civilized norms. It harked back to shams of the Free State days. The judge was ineffectual, clearly influenced by the paranoia of the settlers. The trial, the verdict and the sentence were all miscarriages of justice. So would an execution be. The colonial administration could not make the progress expected of it, if it executed the remarkable Congolese who now and then appeared out of the African population.

The Count recommended that Kimbangu's case be handled with moderation. He believed Kimbangu represented no political threat. He was a spiritual leader, not a political one. The Count acknowledged that settler fears could not be completely ignored. Therefore, he proposed that Kimbangu be rusticated at a good distance from the Bas-Congo for a period of at least five years. He urged that the lashes be suspended.

The Count went so far as to write: "May I take the unusual step of speaking personally?" He explained that on the trip out to the Congo, he resolved not to allow the state to execute innocent men. That Free State practice that must be prohibited. If the palace upheld the sentence condemning Kimbangu to death, he would offer his resignation.

He thought about what he had written for a day, then showed the memo to his wife. "Bravo!" she said. "It's a little strong, but a man's life is at stake." The Count was relieved that she approved what he had written. "You slept clear through last night," she said. "I know this is what you want to say."

The Count showed the draft memo to Van Belle. He read it in the Count's presence and said, "Let me study this. I'll get back to you." That meant his assistant had reservations about what he had written.

Van Belle entered the Governor-General's office the following morning. Ordinarily he moved in it with confidence and familiarity. Now he seemed elaborately careful.

"I read your piece several times," the aide began. "I studied it." The Count said nothing. He would not make it easy for Van Belle to criticize what he had written. The aide would have to spell out his objections.

"It is well-stated, direct, concise. The reader has no confusion about where you stand." Van Belle hesitated, then said carefully, "Early on we agreed to speak to each other frankly." The Count nodded. "If I am to serve you well, I must warn you when I believe that you are-- Well. Courting danger here."

"In what way?"

Van Belle moved his head back and forth, cogitating. "It is very strong," he said.

"Is it?" asked the Count.

"No other Governor-Generals with whom I've worked have addressed the palace in Brussels quite so—" He shrugged.

"A man has been sentenced to death," said the Count.

Van Belle nodded.

"The trial was a sham. The defendant was not represented by counsel. His guilt was assumed from the beginning."

Van Belle said nothing. He moved his head as if to disagree without speaking.

"You see things differently?" asked the Count.

"Some of what you write is, I believe, too personal."

"In what way?"

"You write as a private person. Your advocacy for the defendant suggests a personal relationship. But he is a mere-- I cannot use the word 'citizen.' He's not a citizen. He's charged with sedition." Van Belle spoke with passion, almost as if he were scolding the Count. "You are not a private citizen. You are the Governor-General of the colony. A legal trial held by properly designated colonial officials – which you term a sham – convicted Kimbangu and sentenced him to death."

It surprised the Count to hear his assistant speak these words. He wondered if he had misread Van Belle from the beginning. Unrelenting, he insisted, "It was a sham."

Van Belle avoided confrontation. He looked through the draft document. "It is going too far to say that you will resign if the palace does not spare Kimbangu's life."

"Do you not believe me?"

"I do believe you. And so will the palace. It will be furious. Governor-Generals do not threaten kings."

The Count laughed. He rose from his desk and, as his custom was, began to pace about the office. "I wonder if you have not been as frank with me all these months as I have thought you were."

Van Belle stepped back as if offended. "I have spoken too frankly."

"No!"

"Shall I resign?"

The two men stared at one another. Then the Count laughed. "Are you turning this into melodrama?"

Van Belle measured the Count. At last he smiled. He said, "Not intentionally."

"You cause me to wonder. I thought you were more-- What is the word? Progressive than perhaps you are."

"If you suppose I agree with the Monsignor, sir, that is incorrect. I agree that Belgium's challenge here is to build a-- 'Civilization' is too grand a word. But to build a society—" He shrugged, "A society of some sort. Something better than we have now. But I think it will take generations."

"Certainly it will if we kill off people like Kimbangu."

"I think it is good that you are more-- Is 'enlightened' the word?"

The Count smiled. "We are carefully choosing our words here."

"Yes," agreed Van Belle. Then he continued, "More enlightened than some of the Free Staters who've served as G-G out here. But I am more aware of settler sentiments than you are. Because I live among settlers. I drink with them in the saloons. I go on picnics with them. I look at their daughters and wonder about marrying again."

"I acknowledge that I have little contact with settlers. I'm not sure how we change that."

"The palace can't ignore them."

"Are you suggesting that I do?"

"It's obvious that you and they come from different slices of society." Van Belle smiled, almost mischievously. "You acknowledge that's the case."

The Count nodded.

"If we are to build a society out here, the settlers will be the cement. The palace understands that. We have to be careful of them."

The Count was not sure he agreed with this idea. Surely a Congolese middle class, if one could be built, would act as the cement. But he was not going to argue the point with Van Belle.

The assistant continued, "If the settlers think Kimbangu's people endanger them, we can't ignore that."

The Count began again to pace. Finally he said, "I do not want Kimbangu executed. I will work to see that doesn't happen." Finally he said, "All right. Look again at what I've written. Tone it down and let me see it."

"Yes, sir," said Van Belle. "I hope our discussion hasn't—"

"It hasn't." The Count flicked his hand, a gesture to show that he still trusted Van Belle.

The assistant smiled with relief and left the office, ready to rewrite the memo. The Count returned to his desk, pleased that the problem of the memo was on its way to being resolved.

The memo, outlining the Governor-General's recommendation, as toned down by Van Belle and further revised by the Count, was sent off to the palace in Brussels. Now the colony must await the decision of the palace and, if possible, turn its attention to other matters. This was not easy for Count Lippens. But he resolved not to be a private person when, in fact, he was the Governor-General.

One evening at dinner his wife commented, "You are always preoccupied these days. Should we get you out into the colony? You could go on tour."

"Like royalty of old?" He smiled, a twinkle in his eye. "That might depress me even more."

"We can't have that."

"As soon as I got this job," he said, "do you remember? You concocted a little story about how our life out here would be."

"Did I believe it would be like this?" She laughed, trying to keep the twinkle in his eye. "Surely not."

"We were the heroes of the story."

"Of course," she said merrily. "It was a romance."

"The Governor-General as Prince Charming," he replied, trying to maintain the banter. "Unfortunately we've stepped out of the fairy tale, at least I have."

"So I've noticed, my dear."

"No fairy tales for the G-G. He's the figurehead at the summit of an immense institution that, in stories, is always the villain."

"No, no," she insisted brightly. "It's the palace that's the villain in this story." Since they had finished their dessert, she pulled her chair beside his and took his hand. "I remember a bit of that story now. We promised each other to be discreet. Keep our opinions to ourselves. Cultivate the right people. At the end of the story we went home with our reputations enhanced."

"Which may not be how the story ends now. Even if I bow my head to my sovereign and do whatever Brussels instructs. Will you be disappointed?"

"Not at all." The Countess smiled. "They will think Lippens is quite an amazing fellow. Very sympathetic to the Congolese, which is a plus, but absolutely loyal to the crown." She added, "In my story you don't have to kill anyone."

"Thank you," he said, kissing her hand.

"And we return with our prospects enhanced."

Before any instructions arrived from Brussels, the Count received a communication from Baron Thibaud, the vice-governor in Congo-Kasai. He reported that the prisoner Sambry had escaped from prison, apparently with the help of the very men who had testified against him at his trial.

"Always something new out of Africa," thought the Count. Sambry had apparently made his way to Kinshasa. From there he crossed Stanley Pool to Brazzaville and had by now disappeared into what the French called Moyen-Congo.

"Good riddance," thought the Count. He had no desire to chase the man. Sambry's experience of the Belgian Congo had been uniformly bad. He doubted that he would ever return. Let the French deal with him.

Eventually the palace in Brussels spoke. It commuted Simon Kimbangu's death sentence. Instead he was to be imprisoned for life in the penal colony at Elisabethville in Katanga.

Van Belle stood beside the Count as he read the instructions. "This is what you hoped for, sir. Congratulations." Van Belle was intentionally upbeat for he knew that the Count was disappointed.

"At least Kimbangu will not be executed," noted the Count.

Van Belle did his best to sound optimistic. "Congolese prisons are fairly casual. Kimbangu will probably be free to move around the prison grounds." He added, "I suppose it's possible, even likely, that after, say, five years, ten years, he could be released altogether."

The Count said, "Thank you for bringing me this news. You will take care of the necessary?"

'Yes, sir."

As Van Belle started to leave the room, the Count said, "You remember: I want to see Kimbangu before he's sent to Katanga."

When the Count joined his wife for lunch at the residence, she regarded him sadly and told him, "I heard the news."

"There are no secrets in this place," said the Count.

"The palace must have decided to try to please everyone. Commute the sentence for you. Give the settlers and the Church life imprisonment. No one's left with nothing."

"Yes. Very palatial."

Maybe now, the Count thought, it was time to start thinking about what he would say to Simon Kimbangu. Even though he was not religious, he would like to say something to the prophet that was upbeat, perhaps something of the sort his mother would say.

TWENTY-TWO

O N THE MORNING BEFORE HE WAS TO BE SENT to the Katanga penal colony, a detachment of four armed Congolese guards brought Simon Kimbangu to the seat of the colonial administration. Newly washed himself, the prisoner wore a newly washed tunic and trousers. Manacles curbed the freedom of both his hands and his feet. He walked awkwardly, requiring a quarter of an hour to climb the stairs to the second floor.

Meanwhile Count Lippens sat at his desk, reviewing what he would say to Kimbangu. Since he knew the sight of it would bother his visitor, he had had the nail fetish removed from the office. Finally a knock came at his door. Van Belle entered.

"Simon Kimbangu has arrived," he announced, "accompanied by four guards." The aide studied the Count long enough to perceive his nervousness. "The captain of the guard is reluctant to allow you to see the prisoner alone."

The Count smiled to himself. "I take full responsibility," he said.

"He requests a note to that effect."

As the Count opened a desk drawer, he instructed, "If Kimbangu's manacled, I want the manacles removed." He took a piece of paper from the drawer and wrote a note for the captain of the guard. He folded it and handed it to Van Belle.

The aide withdrew. The Count stood and waited, his hands held behind his back to control them. A knock sounded. Van Belle entered, followed by Kimbangu. "Simon Kimbangu," announced Van Belle.

Kimbangu took several steps into the room and stood. The Count saw immediately that he did not move easily. He was dressed in much the same way as when the two men first met. Even so, the Count noticed that he had been under considerable strain. He had lost weight. The tunic hung on him.

The two men regarded one another. The Count had thought often about what he would say. Still, he was not quite sure how to begin.

Kimbangu gazed at the Count uncertainly. He did not understand why he was there.

Studying the prophet, the Count saw how much incarceration had damaged the man. When they had first met, Count Lippens was surprised to perceive that they were equals in attainment. Each man had risen to high achievement in his field. Each man possessed qualities that credentialed him.

Incarceration had stripped Kimbangu of that achievement and those credentials. Now he was merely a black man, an African prisoner brought before the Governor-General for his inspection. The change, wrought by his administration, embarrassed the Count. If we had gotten him away and kept him under generous house arrest, thought the Count, this would not have happened.

Finally he began, "I wanted to see you before your journey to Katanga." Kimbangu did not react. Like any Congolese prisoner he waited to learn why he had been brought to the Governor-General's office. Intuiting this, the Count gave a small smile and gestured apologetically. "Do you have any idea why you're here?" A longish pause. Kimbangu waited, glancing around the office.

"The fetish is gone," he remarked.

"Yes," said the Count. "I started to talk to it."

"Did it answer you?" The two men smiled.

"The best men in the country say that we must put away fetishes," the Count commented, trying to forge anew the earlier connection.

Kimbangu nodded slightly, aware of what was meant. "I congratulate you," he said.

Since it was proving difficult to achieve rapport, the Count took refuge in what he had described to Van Belle as the official reason for the visit. He said, "You've undoubtedly heard that the King commuted your sentence to life imprisonment."

Kimbangu nodded. He had been apprised of that development.

"Even so, I wanted to tell you myself." Kimbangu did not react. The Count's discomfort deepened. He drew into himself, wanting to connect with Kimbangu as one man reaches out to another. But he realized that this would hardly be possible.

With embarrassment he looked into his visitor's eyes. "I know that an injustice--" he started. "A great injustice has been done--" Because the words were genuine, in speaking them he began to feel comfortable. "To you. That goes without saying. However, it's important that I do acknowledge that to you."

The Count tried to smile. Kimbangu listened. "An injustice has been done to the colony as well." After a moment he added, "Although most of the colonials do not see it that way." He sought some encouragement from Kimbangu, but the man did not react. The Count went on. "Unfortunately, I can do nothing to undo this injustice. Although I am the Governor-General, I am also a creature of the Belgian colonial system."

Kimbangu listened, giving the Count little encouragement.

Because of his embarrassment the Count took refuge in moving about. "These injustices grow out of that system and the fears it engenders." He realized he must be speaking in a manner Kimbangu would not understand. He stopped moving. He turned to his visitor and said simply. "The Belgians are afraid of the Congolese; the Congolese are afraid of the Belgians. That's the fault of this system." The Count wondered: Was he forging any connection with Kimbangu? "Do you understand?" he asked.

"I was surprised when they told me that I was going to see the Governor-General." Kimbangu's reply ignored the Count's embarrassment, his effort to explain. "I was going to tell my jailers that I had nothing to say to you. I could not believe you had anything to say to me." He made an attempt to smile. "I mean: in manacles I understand what you are saying to me."

Taking refuge in formality, the Count said, "I wanted you to hear from my mouth that the death sentence was commuted."

Kimbangu continued on his own track. "Then I realized that if I went to see you at least for a short time they would take off the manacles." He raised his hands and feet to demonstrate his freedom. "They would release me from my prison clothes." He glanced again about the Governor-General's office. He gave a burst of laughter. "It would not be permissible for my prison clothes to smell up the office of the Governor-General." He showed off the fresh clothes and laughed at turning the visit to his advantage. The Count smiled, as much at Kimbangu's amusement as at its meaning.

"For a short time at least I would be put into a tunic and a clean pair of trousers," Kimbangu continued. 'The manacles would come off my wrists and ankles." He rubbed his wrists with his hands, a cherished possibility due to his momentary freedom. "I would walk normally again for a few minutes." He walked back and forth across the office. "Perhaps I would be given a shower." His face lit up with pleasure. He reached out his hands to the Count. "Thanks to you, Governor-General, I was pushed into a hot shower and given half a bar of soap."

Count Lippens took his hands and smiled. "Would you like to sit down?"

"Thank you." The Count led him to one of the easy chairs before his desk. Kimbangu released the Count's grip, lowered his body onto the upholstery, and sat with an expression of sublime pleasure. He luxuriated in the chair. He laughed. "Could we have this chair sent to my cell?"

The Count smiled, but he did not sit. He confessed, "I have never thought of myself as religious." As he embarked on what he intended to tell Kimbangu, he felt a different sort of embarrassment, that of offering advice he had not proved. "Still, I want to remind you that God goes with you on your journey to Katanga." After a moment he added, "That's what my mother told me when I set forth to the Congo."

Kimbangu nodded. "Nzambi has been telling me this very thing."

As if to honor his mother, to act out the etiquette she had taught him, the Count sat in the chair opposite Kimbangu. "My mother was religious," the Count explained. "Where some children heard about Cinderella, I heard Bible stories." He turned directly toward Kimbangu. "My mother would be horrified at what has happened to you here – and while I am directing the colony."

Kimbangu nodded.

"And she would be very distressed at what has happened to me. That I am not, even as Governor-General, able to alter your sentence."

Again Kimbangu nodded.

"She would tell you – and have me tell you - that God is inside whatever kind of uniform they make you wear. Inside the shackles on your ankles and wrists." The Count spoke with his mother's conviction. "God is with you on the train that takes you to Katanga. With you as the lashes are applied to your back. With you in whatever kind of cell they put you in."

How strange this was! the Count felt, hearing himself speak these words. He felt surprised at himself, but he did not feel that what he said was untrue.

"And Nzambi is here with us." Kimbangu said. "Right now." In his eyes shone some of the vitality the Count had remarked when they first met. "Here, in the Governor-General's office!"

The Count smiled with some surprise. Many people, colonials and Congolese alike, would regard that as an improbability.

Kimbangu asked, "Do you believe that?"

The Count accepted that spirituality existed and that there was something like God. He had once informed the Monsignor that God was not an old man in the sky. Rather God was an idea. If an idea, then, of course, he was present with them, as idea, as God and as Nzambi. "Yes, I do believe it," acknowledged the Count.

"Should we talk to Him?" asked Kimbangu.

The Count smiled, a little surprised. Was this an invitation to pray? Did that mean the prophet would start shouting? Goodness! he thought. But he was game. "Yes, let's talk to Him," agreed the Count. "You'll have to show me how."

Kimbangu rose from his chair. The Count followed his lead. The prophet stepped a couple of paces before his chair and started to lower himself to the floor. The Count hurried forward, took his arm, and settled him on his knees. He glanced up at the Count with a look of thanks, with a look of invitation. The Count knelt beside him.

"We will talk to Him silently today," said Kimbangu. "Tell Him what is in your heart."

The prophet closed his eyes. The Count felt that he should also close his and did so. In the darkness behind those eyes, he wondered: What now? Then he further wondered, "Well, what's in your heart?" So he asked Whatever-God-Was to guide Kimbangu, to lead him to a place of safety. It did not occur to him to listen for God's answer so he did not know if an answer came.

After some moments, he felt Kimbangu adjusting himself to rise. The Count quickly stood and, reaching for Kimbangu's arm, helped him to stand. The prophet sat again in his chair. So did the Count.

The Count smiled and, feeling surprisingly at ease, asked, "Did Nzambi speak to you?"

Kimbangu smiled. "He asked me, 'Who is that praying next to you?'"

The Count laughed.

"Nzambi will be with me in Katanga," noted Kimbangu. He spoke as if this were settled truth. He added, "And after I leave here, He will be with you."

"Yes," agreed the Count. It occurred to him that imprisonment might not mean the end of Kimbangu's teaching. The fact of this might disconcert colonials, he thought, but they would dismiss that possibility because they knew he was in prison.

"And since you can never be separated from God," the Count pointed out, "Belgian colonial justice cannot push you apart. You can still do your spiritual work." The Count paused, as if to honor his mother. "That is what my Mother would say." A trace of emotion sounded in his voice. "I pass that along to you as the good counsel of one of the best Belgians."

"Thank you, my brother," said Kimbangu. "And you believe it, too?"

The Count nodded, feeling that perhaps some connection had been made, that for a moment they were equals again. "I am sorry that you cannot take that chair with you."

"Yes, Governor-General. It would look good in my cell."

"Have you been told that the Belgian authorities have sent prophets from your church to penal colonies all over the colony? They did not consult me; they just did it."

"I have been told," said Kimbangu

"Those prophets are spreading your religion throughout Central Africa," said the Count. That the administration should facilitate what it wanted suppressed struck the Count as a typical failure of the Belgian colonial system. But it would please Kimbangu. "Take that with you," he told his visitor. "That's better than the chair."

The men rose from their chairs. The Count offered his hand. Kimbangu took it and shaking it placed both of his hands over it.

"This is the arm?" Kimbangu asked.

"Yes. This is it. Thank you."

"Thank you for seeing me," Kimbangu said. "And thank your mother for her wisdom. It applies to you as well – in your prison."

The Count went to the door, opened it slightly, and called for Van Belle. The aide entered and escorted Kimbangu out of the office.

The Count stood for a moment, gazing into the chair Kimbangu had occupied, then returned to his desk to resume his work. Sitting again, he thought that whatever other meetings he might have in the Belgian Congo, this one would probably be the most significant of his time as Governor-General.

AFTERWORD

THE BELGIAN CONGO SPENT THE EARLY MIDDLE years of the twentieth century in a kind of hibernation. It was as if the heat, the humid air, the vegetation, and the endless round of wet and dry seasons lulled the entire colony to sleep. A war raged in faraway Europe. Africans fought in that war. The war and their fighting changed the course of the way things were. Africans demanded independence, and governments exhausted by war granted it to them.

After seventy-five years of colonial rule, the Belgian Congo was to accede to independence on June 30, 1960. In spring of that year a group of Flemish and Dutch real estate investors weighed the prospects for the colony's independence as a sovereign nation and decided that it might be possible to pick up cheap land holdings that could prove valuable in, say, twenty or thirty years.

They sent Paul Janssens to Léopoldville to check out these prospects on the ground. Janssens invited his wife Annette to accompany him. She was delighted to accept. Growing up, she had heard tales of the far-off Congo. Her grandfather Hugo's brother-in-law Maurice Count Lippens had served as Governor-General of the colony some forty years before.

M. and Mme Janssens flew to the Congo on Sabena, the Belgian national airline. They stayed at the Memling Hotel in downtown Léopoldville. During the days while her husband met with plantation owners and government officials, some of them interesting, some of them not so much, Annette Janssens visited African markets, curio shops, and folk art museums.

Most of the men Paul Janssens met recounted tales of early years of hardship and adventure. Most of them warned that the Congo was ill-prepared for independence. Too few Congolese had achieved the kind of education to run a country so vast and potentially so wealthy. The perspectives of most Congolese remained tribal. Belgium's Société Génerale had done a good job of developing and exploiting the mining assets in the country's southeast. But in the rest of the country infrastructure that could bind the regions together was lacking.

Mme Janssens heard many of these analyses at the dinners she attended with her husband. She became bored and restless. She had hoped the trip would provide some connection with her great uncle. But that was not the case. She learned that Count Lippens and his Countess had never lived in Léopoldville, the capital. They had resided at a place called Boma at the estuary of the great river. Perhaps she should have realized that, but she hadn't.

When her husband announced that he must visit land holdings in the interior, places that would be of no interest to her, she said, "I think I'll fly down to Boma to take a look around."

Her husband seemed surprised. "Is that a good idea?" he asked. "Will you be safe?"

She cocked an eyebrow and replied, "Do you really think I'm safe here while you're away? In fact, I'm quite bored."

It crossed his mind to suggest that she return to Ghent where they had left their children in the care of a trusted nanny. But he thought that such a response might only trigger the reactions that could cause a bored woman to get into trouble. So he said, "I think that's an excellent idea. You can tell the whole family what you learned when we get home."

When Paul Janssens headed to the Kivu on the country's eastern frontier, Annette took an Air Congo flight to Boma. She found the town quite small and very sleepy. She checked into a rustic hotel, sustained by colonials who came to drink at its bar. They were delighted to encounter a fresh face, to relate stories and dire predictions like those she had already heard in the capital.

A single woman from the metropole, a woman of some refinement – Mme Janssens had no ability or reason to hide what she obviously was – seemed a great curiosity in Boma, especially with the colony on the cusp of such change. She let it be known that her great uncle had been a Governor-General of the colony. For good measure she modestly mentioned that later he had also served as president of the Belgian Senate. She supposed this candor might be a way of letting her background work as a kind of protective shield.

It also worked as a way of opening doors. The proprietor of her hotel told her, "You should talk with Willem Van Belle. He shepherded maybe a dozen Gov-Gens through their stints."

Annette found where M. Van Belle lived and went to talk with him. In his early seventies and house-bound by illness, he chatted with her about his past services with the string of men who had served as Governors-General. But she quickly discerned that while she was interested in Governor-General Lippens, his recollections had grouped them all indiscriminately into a single holding tank. His memories could no longer sort them out, one from another.

At Van Belle's home, she met the child of his middle years, his son Philippe, perhaps twenty. When they were together, Philippe attempted to sort out his father's memories. An African girl served them beer.

At length Philippe inquired, "Would you like to see the office where the Gov-Gens worked?" Annette was uncertain how to answer. Would that give her some connection to her great uncle Maurice? "That's the girl's idea," said Philippe. He nodded toward the kitchen into which the girl had disappeared. Earlier Annette had detected vibes between her and Philippe. Now she wondered about a romantic attachment between them.

As much to encourage that attachment as for any interest in the office, she said, "Yes, I'd like very much to see it." They arranged a time to meet at the former State House. As Annette left, she made a special display of thanking the African girl. Saying goodbye to Philippe, she asked, "Will she come with us?"

"Perhaps," he said.

But when they met the next day the girl was not with Philippe. When Annette asked if she would be joining them, Philippe said simply, "No." He explained, "She has duties at the house."

Philippe greeted the guards who tended the former State House, led Annette through the former entry hall and up the staircase. "This was my father's office," he explained, leading her through an empty room. He opened a door onto a large space. "This is it," he said as they entered the former office of the Governors-General. "Rather stuffy in here."

Indeed, the room smelled as if it had been closed for a very long time. The furniture was covered with protective sheets. The walls were blank, but there were rectangles where paintings or photographs had hung.

"Let me take up these so you can get a sense of the place." Philippe pulled sheets off the furniture: a desk, two easy chairs and a sofa. He wadded up the sheets and tossed them into a corner.

"We're pretty casual for this place," he remarked. "In its day the men who had audiences with a Gov-Gen wore white suits and carried pith helmets." Philippe stroked his clean-shaven chin. He had close-cropped hair and wore jeans, a polo shirt, and sandals. Annette had dressed in slacks and a blouse, her hair pulled back in a ponytail. "Most of them had huge mustaches," Philippe went on. "Some men waxed them, if you can imagine. And some even had white shoes."

Annette thanked the young man for removing the sheets and looked about the room. She noticed a very large rectangle on the wall behind the desk and wondered what had hung there.

Philippe said, "Quite a grand office in its day, I believe."

"My great-aunt used to talk about this room," Annette observed. "The Count did not serve as Governor-General all that long." Philippe had such casual manners that it seemed stuffy to call Uncle Maurice the Count, but she didn't know how else to refer to him.

"I'm sorry my father's not up to taking you around," Philippe said. "He ought to remember a Count. But it's very easy to get things confused. Is he the one that tripped on stairs one night and broke his arm?"

"He did break his arm," Annette said. "I'm not sure I ever knew how."

Philippe did not immediately reply. Annette wondered if it was to see if she would acknowledge how it was healed. "Did it heal okay?" he finally asked. "Sometimes in the tropics…"

Again the moment of silence. Then Philippe commented, "There's talk of turning this place into a hospital at independence." More silence. "The expectations of the Congolese are over the moon."

Annette finally felt courageous. Who would ever know they had talked? "The story in the family is that the broken arm was healed by an African—"

"A witchdoctor?" Philippe cried. He laughed heartily. But behind the laughter she felt he studied her, testing her forthrightness.

"An African prophet. A man called Simon Kimbangu." Annette felt relieved that she had not been afraid to mention the healing. "We tend to keep that inside the family. In Belgium people—"

Philippe nodded. "Dear little Belgium."

Annette did not want to discuss Europe. "When was the seat of government transferred to Léopoldville?" she asked. "That was after the Count's time. They spent their whole two years down here."

Philippe thought for a moment. "Maybe 1925, 26?"

"Your people chose to stay here?"

Philippe laughed. The testing had passed. "We weren't 'people' yet. My father decided to leave the colonial service," he explained. "All his contacts were here. He knew everyone, all the chiefs. Spoke the language. Had a house and a circle of friends and decided to stay."

Annette wondered if he also had a woman, but thought it indelicate to ask. Philippe looked at her as if he knew what she was wondering. He was not forthcoming.

"Papa took a job with a Belgian transport company. It moved its headquarters to Léo, but needed a good man here in Boma."

Annette plunged ahead. "He found a wife down here?"

"No, no. He went to the metropole in 1930. He was forty-two." There must have been a Congolese woman, Annette thought. "We tease him that he went to Belgium over forty and asked every woman he met under thirty-five if she would please please marry him and come live with him on the Congo River estuary." He laughed heartily. "They would say, 'The Congo! Ehk! You must be insane.' Finally he found a widow with two children and they came out."

"And are they still here?"

"His first wife died. The widow. The kids went back to the metropole." Philippe shrugged. "So he went back again and found my mother. They had me." Philippe looked around the room. Annette was about to ask if his mother was still in the

Congo, but before she could, he asked, "What brings you to Boma right now?"

"My husband has business to transact in Léo prior to independence."

"What kind of business?"

"He's looking into land holdings people might want to sell."

Philippe studied her with new interest as if she had suddenly become a different person to him. He gave a laugh. "There must be quite a few of those, people who don't want to risk what it'll be like here in a year." He examined her. "Your husband's willing to take a chance, eh?"

"I think maybe it'll be a great success." She had learned to say this because it was what her husband's investors expected of her.

"Really?" Philippe said. Now he regarded her as if she were, after all, the woman he thought she must be. "Tiny Belgium has been a disaster as a colonial power," he informed her. "You know that, right? Thought it could develop the colony in isolation from the territories around it, in isolation from what was happening in the world. Where did it get that idea?" He measured her, waiting for her to speak. She smiled. He added, "Now it's handling the end of colonialism as badly as everything else it's done. What a balls up!"

"You're a man who speaks his mind."

He smiled at her rather gently. "My apologies if I offend you. But the truth is: the preparations for independence are a disaster."

"Truly?"

"There aren't enough educated Congolese to organize a card game, much less a country."

"Are you staying?"

"Leaving the first of May."

"For the metropole?"

"Not a chance. Belgium is small enough to hold in your hand. When you've lived in a place as big as the Congo, who'd go there?"

Annette sat in an easy chair. This room seemed to be the extent of the tour. "Where then?" she asked.

"Canada. Montreal. I did a year of university there."

"And your parents?"

"I keep urging them to join me. Papa knows this place will be a mess. But he's seventy-two. No moving for him."

Philippe took a seat in the easy chair opposite her and stretched his legs out before him. "So your husband's looking at what? Land that planters are trying to offload? Failing plantations?"

"He seems to think proper management will make a difference."

"Let's hope he's right."

Annette felt emboldened to ask, "What can you tell me about Simon Kimbangu?"

Philippe smiled. "I've been sitting here, trying to place which Gov-Gen your great uncle must have been. He was the one who was damned if they'd make him execute an African healer who did nothing but give the settlers a good scare." He looked squarely at Annette. "He doesn't talk about that?"

"Not his game."

"He doesn't mention, 'Squash the bug'?"

Annette frowned. "What's that?"

"That's what the high mucky-muck of the Catholic Church urged your great-uncle to do. Kimbangu was the bug. These were the men who were absolving us of our sins!" Philippe laughed. "Your great uncle wanted to whisk Kimbangu away to a place of safety up the river. Real spy-novel stuff. My father was appalled." Philippe laughed and Annette joined him. "He wanted to tell the king he'd resign if Kimbangu was executed. A Governor-General challenging a king. That made my father sweat."

"My great-uncle did that? He was such a steady person."

"Anyway Kimbangu was spared," he said. "Papa was on the wrong side of that one."

"You have strong opinions," Annette observed, smiling.

"In a place like this there's no point in having mild ones! Papa takes a generous view of things. People generally try to do the best they can, he says. I say, 'Bullshit!' It gives us something to talk about at dinner."

Annette laughed, thinking those conversations might be fun to witness. She asked, "Wasn't Kimbangu sentenced to prison?"

"To death! Then that was commuted. My father says the conflict between political power and transcendence can never be fully resolved. That make sense to you?"

Annette shrugged.

"He says Kimbangu represented transcendence bursting on the scene like a Second Coming – and challenging the colonial administration. That tension is never resolved, says my father which art not in heaven." Philippe grinned. He rose and began walking about the room. "Never resolved in this world. Not in our lives."

Annette smiled. "I'm not sure my great uncle ever resolved it," she said, "He resigned after two years. Disagreements with the Ministry of Colonies."

"About what?" Philippe asked.

Annette shook her head. "I've no idea. He may have been too liberal. It's a liberal family."

"Have you heard this?" Philippe asked. "Kimbangu ran away when he first heard God talking to him." Annette shook her head. "Probably a very intelligent reaction since he paid a terrible price for doing what God told him to do."

"Was Kimbangu in solitary confinement?"

"No, no. I don't think so." Philippe stopped walking and sat on the edge of the Governor-General's desk. "Africans don't do solitary very well. Prisons are fairly casual."

"Still they are prisons," observed Annette.

"Yes. And they must thwart healing powers. To have his healing powers diminished must have been a terrible price for Kimbangu to pay."

"Were they diminished?"

"Isn't that the point of prison? Everything's diminished."

"Did the teachings die out?"

"No, no. Eventually his son Joseph Diangienda took over. There was a queen mother, too."

Annette smiled at this irreverence.

Philippe went to the pile of sheets he had tossed aside. He took one, opened it with a vigorous shake and let it settle over the desk. "The word made flesh," he said. "An amazing gift. Kimbangu was the real thing."

Annette watched the young man take another sheet and shake it out. She wondered how, if prison diminished his spiritual powers, Kimbangu could have been what Philippe regarded as "the real thing."

Philippe settled the sheet over the easy chair in which he sat. As if reading her mind he said, "Kimbangu's ideas, his teachings if you can call them that: they've helped countless people."

"Really?"

"He and the prophets in his movement kept proselytizing from prison. What else would you expect from a Belgian colonial prison system?"

Annette smiled uncertainly. "I don't understand."

"When Kimbanguism got started—"

Annette interrupted. "You said 'ism.' Is there an 'ism'?"

Philippe laughed. "Yes, there is. When it started, there were prophets popping up all around. The *n'gunza*, they were called. The authorities rusticated them to penal colonies throughout the Congo. There they served as missionaries. Isn't that a laugh?" Philippe guffawed heartily. "White man thinks he's suppressing the movement. Black man knows he's spreading it. Black man figures if the *n'gunza* had to be rusticated, they must have special knowledge. So they listen to them."

Annette was amused at the young man's evident pleasure in relating the administration's folly. He took another sheet. Annette left her chair so that he could cover it.

"The real joke is Kimbangu turned out to be a genuine holy man," Philippe said. "No one in the colonial administration or the Church realized that. They were too busy getting everything wrong." He glanced at her sympathetically. "I'm not talking about your great uncle, you understand. He went full out for him."

"A genuine holy man?" she asked. "I don't understand."

"There's a Kimbanguist church," Philippe said. "Very active around here."

"It wasn't suppressed then?"

"No, no. It has some twenty million members, some as far away as Europe."

"My great-uncle died four years ago. Is Kimbangu still alive?"

"He died about a decade ago. Maybe 1951? He was at the penal colony for thirty years."

"A long time to languish."

"Yes," agreed Philippe. "Rusticating prophets, making them missionaries: that's a very Belgian way of suppressing a religion. Kimbangu must have died smiling." They glanced around the room. "I guess we're finished here," said Philippe.

They passed through the office that Philippe's father had used and went out into the hall. Annette started down the staircase.

Once outside she said, "I think I'll walk about a while. Thank you so much for the tour." She and Philippe shook hands.

"May your husband find many properties worth the purchase."

"May you prosper in Canada."

They said goodbye and started off in different directions.

Annette walked down by the river. She thought of her great uncle. He had come to the Congo just after the Free State era when maiming and killing Congolese was routine. But the way the story was told in the family, Maurice Count Lippens had changed that. Because of him, Kimbangu's death sentence was lifted. In a sense great uncle Maurice had made it possible for a kind of second coming to occur. How truly extraordinary Africa was!

Why Did I Write Congo Prophet?

In 1963 in my late 20s, I was sent to the Congo, three years into its chaotic independence. I went to serve as an American Foreign Service Officer for the United States Information Service. I had just come off a nine-month training stint in Brussels, Belgium, and knew nothing about Africa – except that independence had gotten a very bad start in the Congo. So bad a start, in fact, that officers who had pledged to serve anywhere in the world were resigning from USIS and the State Department in preference to serving in the Congo. Although I was just off an indoctrination post and knew nothing, I was sent to Coquilhatville in the remote northwest of the country to open a post, an American cultural center. Needless to say, in a smooth running State Department an officer just off a training post is not sent to a place like the Congo to open a post.

Naturally once I more or less settled in, I asked myself questions: "What in the world are we Americans doing here? Do the local people really need an American cultural center?" One answer to such questions was the Belgian colonial answer: "We are despoiling these people of their riches." Other answers, provided by American officials were: "We are making sure these people vote with us in the UN. Or: We are in a to-the-death fight with the Russians, and we are making damn sure they do not get a foothold in Central Africa."

But these answers did not satisfy a liberal-arts, college-educated idealist who was likely several decades later to write a novel about a Governor-General of the Congo Free State who had been sent out from Belgium to set things right. In part my answer to that question was: "We are here to help the Congolese navigate the modern world, a place very different from what they have known in their villages." Nation-building was not a scorned enterprise in the 1960s and I was all in for it.

At some point during my time in the Congo I read about Simon Kimbangu. He seemed a person – probably an authentic holy man – who was trying to do the same sort of thing I was, but from a very different perspective using a very different set of tools. I also read about Maurice Count Lippens, the newly arrived Belgian Governor-General, who had to confront the problem that Kimbangu represented. Many Belgian interests – church, estate managers, small business people, settlers, bureaucrats – wanted him tried and executed – for being a holy man. Lippens did his best to oppose them. But eventually he was overwhelmed. Kimbangu was given a show trial, convicted, and sentenced to death.

This historical narrative seemed to parallel another story out of history with which I was familiar: Pontius Pilate's dilemma of what to do about Jesus. That truly fascinated me. I kept the story of Kimbangu and Lippens at the back of my mind for several decades. Once I started looking into it, the Internet speeded the process of research. And in writing other novels about Africa, I had learned how to put my imagination to use.

Congo Prophet is an amalgam of both historical and imaginative elements. My Count Lippens is, I suppose, much more of a 21st Century governor-general than would have been a man sent to Boma in 1921, even if his job was to set things aright. The same is probably true of Kimbangu, whose religion survives today.

Looking back at *Congo Prophet,* I am left with the overwhelming cruelty that survived the worst abuses of the past yet nevertheless tainted the "modern day" efforts at reform made by Maurice Lippens.

Why couldn't the Belgian administration let Simon live in freedom?

—Frederic Hunter

About Cune Press

Cune Press was founded in 1994 to publish thoughtful writing of public importance. Our name is derived from "cuneiform." (In Latin *cuni* means "wedge.")

In the ancient Near East the development of cuneiform script—simpler and more adaptable than hieroglyphics—enabled a large class of merchants and landowners to become literate. Clay tablets inscribed with wedge-shaped stylus marks made possible a broad inter meshing of individual efforts in trade and commerce.

Cuneiform enabled scholarship to exist and art to flower, and created what historians define as the world's first civilization. When the Phoenicians developed their sound-based alphabet, they expressed it in cuneiform.

The idea of Cune Press is the democratization of learning, the faith that rarefied ideas, pulled from dusty pedestals and displayed in the streets, can transform the lives of ordinary people. And it is the conviction that ordinary people, trusted with the most precious gifts of civilization, will give our culture elasticity and depth—a necessity if we are to survive in a time of rapid change.

Books from Cune Press

 Aswat: Voices from a Small Planet (a series from Cune Press)

Looking Both Ways	Pauline Kaldas
Stage Warriors	Sarah Imes Borden
Stories My Father Told Me	Helen Zughaib & Elia Zughaib
Girl Fighters	Carolyn Han

 Syria Crossroads (a series from Cune Press)

Leaving Syria	Bill Dienst & Madi Williamson
Visit the Old City of Aleppo	Khaldoun Fansa
Stories My Father Told Me	Helen Zughaib, Elia Zughai
Steel & Silk	Sami Moubayed
Syria - A Decade of Lost Chances	Carsten Wieland
The Road from Damascus	Scott C. Davis
A Pen of Damascus Steel	Ali Ferzat
White Carnations	Musa Rahum Abbas

 Bridge Between the Cultures (a series from Cune Press)

Empower a Refugee	Patricia Martin Holt
Biblical Time Out of Mind	Tom Gage, James A. Freeman
Turning Fear Into Power	Linda Sartor
The Other Side of the Wall	Richard Hardigan
Apartheid Is a Crime	Mats Svensson
Curse of the Achille Lauro	Reem al-Nimer
Arab Boy Delivered	Paul A. Zarou

 Cune Cune Press: www.cunepress.com | www.cunepress.net

FREDERIC HUNTER SERVED AS A Foreign Service Officer in the United States Information Service in Brussels, Belgium, and, shortly after its independence, at three posts in the Republic of the Congo: Bukavu, Coquilhatville, and Léopoldville. He later became the Africa Correspondent of the *Christian Science Monitor*, based in Nairobi.

A playwright / screenwriter, Hunter's award-winning stage work, The *Hemingway Play*, was given a reading at the Eugene O'Neill Playwrights Conference, presented at Harvard University's Loeb Drama Center and produced by PBS's Hollywood Television Theater series. Other plays have been performed at the Dallas Theatre Center, ACT in San Francisco, and the Ensemble Theater in Santa Barbara.

Movies Hunter has written have been produced by PBS, ABC, and CBS. Research for his PBS drama *Lincoln and the War Within* led him to write the historical novel *Abe and Molly: The Lincoln Courtship*. He's taught screenwriting at the Santa Barbara Writers Conference, at UCSB, and at Principia College where he also taught Modern African Literature. Hunter's Africa experience is the basis for ten current and forthcoming novels and short story collections from Cune Press.

Fred Hunter blogs at www.TravelsinAfrica.com.

CPSIA information can be obtained
at www.ICGtesting.com
Printed in the USA
JSHW061424160922
30598JS00003B/3